AF540295

Myths and Symbols in W.B. Yeats

Myths and Symbols in W.B. Yeats

Professor (Dr.) Samrendra Sharma

Myths and Symbols in W.B. Yeats

Edition 2024

ISBN 978-93-87537-50-7

Published by:
CRESCENT PUBLISHING CORPORATION
4806/24, Mathur Lane,
Ansari Road, Darya Ganj,
New Delhi - 110 002
Ph.: 011 - 23244131
Mob.: + 91 - 9711991838, 9999021668
E-mail: crescentbook@gmail.com
Website: www.crescentpublishingcorp.weebly.com

Printed at:
Roshan Offset Printers
Delhi

Acknowledgements

No work of research and ultimately making a book out of that is possible but for the help of those persons who are around you and keep the flame of pursuit alive by providing persistent encouragement. This book on the topic Myths and Symbols in W.B Yeats. Has become a possibility due to the accumulated impact of certain persons who disciplined my intellect for the longest journey.

I am deeply indebted to Dr Tejinder Kaur of Panjabi University Patiala who kept me guiding me for tracing the Genesis of Yeats' myths and symbols in Indian Mythology and history. Without her help the book would remain an impossibility.

I am thankful to my colleagues in the department of English who initiated me on the path of delving deep in the realm of literature and encouraged me to always to revive my thinking and morale.

I am thankful to my wife Mrs Pankaj and children Aarushi and Rakesh who remained very cooperative during preparation of this book. I am highly thankful to my parents Smt. Raj Rani and Sh. Kidar Nath Sharma who are the real source of inspiration for me to do any task in life.

I am thankful to the publisher Crescent Publishing Corporation, Darya Ganj, New Delhi.

Thanks to Almighty God.

Preface

W.B. Yeats popularity mostly rests on the use of myth and symbol. He has abundantly borrowed myth from religion, primitive folklore. Greek Mythology and Irish Mythology. The forces of nature and change of civilization have been raised at the level of supernatural occurrence in his poems. By means of symbol, something concrete - an object, a place, a character, an action–something concrete stands for something abstract, W.B.Yeats has concretized vague, fleeting sensations and experiences in his poems. Myth is a kind of traditional and anonymous story. It is a means to give cultural and social customs of human and natural phenomena, usually in supernatural or imaginative terms. Myth is supposed to be a false or unreliable story . But it is a superior intuitive mode of cosmic understanding. In most literary contexts, intuitive mode of cosmic understanding prevails because myths are deeper truths, expressing collective attitudes to fundamental matters of life, death, divinity and existence. In classical Greek, "myths" signified any story or plot, whether true or invented. In its central modern significance, however, a myth is one story in a mythology– a system of hereditary stories of ancient origin which were once believed to be true by a particular cultural group, and which served to explain why the world is as it is and things happen as they do, to provide a rationale for social customs and observances, and to establish the sanctions for the rules by which people conduct their lives. Myths lack the historical framework of legend and moral teaching of fables. However it does not mean that it is completely fictitious.

The only reason is that myths are less historical than legend. Even if people no longer believe in the true existence of mythical situation, myths are related to social rituals as well. Mythical stories are supernatural tales that are deliberately invented by their authors. Jeremy Hawthorn analytically presents the conceptual meaning of myth," In recent usage, then, the concepts of myth and of ideology are interlinked: myths perform an ideological function while ideologies function by means of myths. . Hawthorn shows the interrelation of myths and ideologies since both are the belief systems that operate on the basis of shared views. Myths cannot be called only the production of creative imagination rather they are related to the archetypal experiences of the race, birth, mating and death. W.B. Yeats's monkish hatred for science and mounting ugliness and barrenness of an industrial civilization, his consciousness of the conflict and tensions of human life, the awareness of the passing away of beauty and his love for Maud Gonne made him the lover of myth and symbol. The poems "The Second Coming", "Leda and the Swan" and " A Prayer for My Daughter" illustrate the myth-making habit of the poet. His mythopoetic imagination modifies and transforms old myths. Further, his Symbolism is fully and firmly grounded in Greek Mythology and Irish Mythology. This imparts precision, a definition, a clear lucidity and pictorial quality in his poetry. The symbols of Yeats are all-pervasive. There are certain symbols like Byzantium, rose, tower, swan, the sword and so on round which a number of poems are arranged, and each poem that follows in succeeding order throws light on foregoing ones and illuminates their sense.

Contents

CHAPTER – I

FORMATIVE INFULNECE ON YEATS

W.B.Yeats (1865–1939) was an English poet of great distinction. He started writing poetry from the age of 19 years onward. His father, John Butler Yeats, being himself an artist, drew his sensitive son towards art and literature. Being given to a sensitive frame of mind, he developed interest in mysticism, myths, folk- lore and religion. In this respect he was unlike other children. For Victorian science and for realism in art he conceived what he calls, a monkish hate.

It is his poetic sensibility that made him conscious of his Irish heritage. This awareness in him developed in course of years made his work for Irish literary Revival. Thus Irish folklore and myths inspired him to study past symbols and religious beliefs. In the years as he came across and religious beliefs. In the years as he came across eminent people of diverse interests, he absorbed in his mental make-up thoughts and feelings of other cultures. He did so without being blown off his feet. In this way, he was able to deepen his Irish sensibility: and through his assiduous efforts, as he developed universality in his outlook, he was able to impart a prismatic glitter to his poetry, drama and criticism.

It is on the basis of this background that he came to command a world-wide respect as a poet, dramatist critic and letter-writer. He has a sure touch of language, in poetry as also in prose. He expressed his thoughts with vibrant clarity. He laboured hard to arrive at this felicity of expression without losing the poetic feel he was born with. No wonder T.S. Eliot, who happens to be one of the literary giants of modern literature, chose to adjudge W.B. Yeats as "the greatest poet of our time— Certainly the greatest in this language, and so far as I am able to judge, in any language."

The immense prestige and popularity of Yeats arises because in his poetry and prose there is a deeper commitment towards human life. Even as in his writings he is drawn to the emotive side of human life, he does not go away from reality. Another astonishing aspect of Yeats is that even though he did not have regular institutional education, he made his way to get a kaleidoscopic awareness of life and letters through this open-mindedness and tireless industry.

And Yeats never went to a University. H was able to function in a broad way, an eclectic way, without being an increasingly narrow specialist. He read widely, he read with enthusiasm, he read with feel-ing and found what he wanted, and he had a God-given flair for discovering it. He knew what to look for. Had he gone through a narrow University discipline, we would probably not have had our great poet, .nor, as someone said, our essayist and our playwrigh.

Whatever the formal education he got, it was at the Godolphin School in Hammersmith, London, Apparently, he did not make any spectacular academic progress at this school partly because he also visited Ireland during vaction. Irish surroundings exercised a lingering spell on the poetic sensibility of Yeats. Precisely, he developed at this period of schooling 'an acute sense of his 'Irishness', drawing constant unfavorable comparisons between his idyllic holidays in Sligo and the grinding monotony of school, between the richness of the folklore and mythology he picked up in Ireland and the drabness of formal lessons."

His interest in Irish folklore developed into a life-long absorbing pursuit to understand myths and symbols not only of Ireland but also of other countries. His single- minded pursuit of various myths and symbols helped him to enrich his poetry and drama in style as well as in terms of content. Yeats was able to arrive at artistic excellence because he studied and assimilated various streams of thought and philosophy. English language and literature exercised an abiding influence on Yeats even as he disliked England as an Irish Patriot. This ambivalence engendered in him a dialectical tension arising out of his love for English language and literature counterpoised by his intense aversion for English politics. Once, he acknowledged:

All my family names are English, and.... I owe my soul to Shakespeare, to Spenser, and to Blake, perhaps to william Morris, and to the English language in which I think, speak, and write......, everything I love has come to me through English.

At the same time, his aversion for England comes on the surface of his consciousness over the persecution of the Irish by English people.

'There are moments when hatred poisons my life and I accuse myself of effeminacy because I have not given it adequate expression. .... My hatred tortures me with love, my love with hate.

This ambivalence of Yeats for England was life-lasting and at the same time quite influential, in the sense that of reaction to certain aspects of the English insularity in literary forms, Yeats turned to European poets and dramatists. For example, in building up the Irish National Theatre, Yeats drew much sustenance from the European drama. In the same way, Yeats reacted sharply to the narrow interpretation put by the Victorian realism in literature.

It is on the basis of his emotive sensitiveness Yeats was influenced by his family members, writers and artists. Yeast's liking for different disciplines knowledge was also determined by his emotive response. Since Yeats had a highly receptive mind, he was interested in a host of topics, themes and subjects. To recount them would mean overshadowing certain essential aspects of Yeats in terms of a poet and dramatist; it would therefore be desirable to refer only to those influences which have played a perceptible role in Yeats's literary life. A passing discussion of various influences is to be patterned on the basis of Yeasts' own comments:

(1) Home: In nourishing Yeasts' sensibility, the role of his grandfather is considerable. His grans father, William Pollexfen – on his mother's side, delighted and nervous Yeats by narrating heroic sea stories. He has acknowledged that the larger-than-life figures of his grand father had a permanent effect on him.

Even today when I read King Lear, his image is always before me, and I often wonder if the delight in passionate men in my plays and in my poetry is more than memory.

This observation implies that Yeats developed a feel for life and its grandeur other than the common-place one. In some respects, the influence of his father is no less important. His literary and artistic awareness was greatly sharpened by his father, John Butler Yeats (who used to read him passages from Scott, Homer, Chaucer and Balzac.Then again, it was John Butler Yeats who transmitted to his son ideas of 'Pre-Raphaelitismi. To a very great extent, W.B Yeats derived the habit of free thinking and the spirit of rebelliousness from his father.

Yeats remained influenced by the eminent literary personages introduced to him by his father. Of course, Homer and Balzac influenced Yeats more. In his poems, he availed the Homeric background. For example, in 'The Rose of the world' Deirdre and Helen seemed to co-exist and Helen became the definite figure in 'The Sorrow of Love' Apart from Celtic myths, he all along bore in mind the contribution of Homer and Dante in saving the European civilization from redundancy.

Influenced as he was greatly by the versatility of Balzac in portraying man and society in France in the early part of the nineteenth century with great fidelity to the subtle processes at work, Yeats appreciably commented on the viable scenario created try this great French novelist: '...there in the crowded theatre are Balzac's readers and his theme, seen with his eyes they have become philosophy without ceasing to be history.'

Yeats was greatly charmed by Balzac's gallery of living characters. Apparently bearing in mind the fusion of life and philosophy in a creative mind like Balzac, Yeats held to the argument that the poet had to convey, not 'abstract truth' but 'a kind of vision of reality', as he wrote to his father in 1914, 'which satisfies the whole being'.

In terms of his own art-perspective, Yeats found Balzac's approach congenially and in this frame of mind, he assigned a higher role for an artist than that of a religionist. Viewpoint is that the artist just cannot allow himself to be to absorbed in religion particularly in 'Asiatic vague immensities' whenever I have been tempted to go to Japan, China or India for my philosophy, Balzac has brought me back, reminded me, of my preoccupation with national social, personal, problems, convinced me that I cannot escape from our Comedie Humaine and in the European past, all human destiny'. Yeats considered it of greater significance than that of his own visualization in his prestigious essay, **A Vision.** For Yeats, the artistic vision of a Balzac or a Dante was of theatrical intricacy and completeness, just as it was manifold in its growth and symbolical ordering. It was sustaining, too, as a life-illusion'. This comment has a strident applicability to Yeats's thinking. The art should give verisimilitude of reality in all its dynamic symphony. This is what Balzac did in his **Comedie Humaine;** and this is what Yeats aspired after; and that he succeeded amply well in terms of his poems and dramas.

(ii) **Folklore:** Yeats, influenced as he was much cy the Irish folklore, tried to understand the folklore traditions, not only of Ireland, but also of other countries; and in this intellectual venture, he committed himself to a serious study of myths and mysticism. — in terms of mystic framework, he acquainted himself with Hinduism, Theosophy, Buddhism, literature of Cabbalists and Rosicrucians. In the sphere of literary pursuits, he was receptive to the ideas of French symbolists along with several eminent literary personalities of Europe; Blake, Shelley, Wilde, Swift, Parnell, Milton and above all Shakespeare from English literature and Irish History.

Here, a reference may be made to George Russell (AE) and W.T. Hortonwho have contributed a great deal in deepening and sharpening Yeats's interest in myths, mysticism and Occultism. Yeats was drawn to the study of Irish folklore partly on account of patriotism and partly on account of his instinctive liking for idyllic traditions. Recalling his time at the school of Art in Autobiographies, Yeats speaks of his youthful convictions 'that only beautiful things should be painted, and that only ancient things and the stuff of dreams were beautiful' To feed his dream-oriented visionary outlook, folk-stories sustained him so much so that he incorporated them in his poems. For example, the folk-story that he uses in his poem 'The Old Pensioner' was based upon a narration of the factual story of an old peasant narrated by George Russell (AE) while he was walking on Two Rock Mountain with John Hughes. The old peasant with deep feeling tells Russell and his friend about his wanderings in a particular hilly tract some 40 years earlier; then in the course of narration, he repeated short, concentrated, clipped expression: 'The fret is on me. The fret is on me.' Yeats's poem, 'The old-Pensioner' is reproduced here to show the link between the folklore of Ireland and Yeats's poetry:

I had a chair at every hearth,
When nominee turned to see
With 'Look at that old fellow there,
And who may be?"
And therefore do I wander on,
And the fret is on me.

The roadside trees keep murmuring
Ah, wherefore murmer ye
As in the old days long gone by,
Green oak and polar tree
The well-known faces are all gone,
And the fret is on me.

Yeats re-enlivens the lonely, fretful life of the old peasant and the period in which he lived. This poem Marks the interfusion of diverse folklore elements that impart gravity with suffused pathos to Yeats's poetry. This assessment is also underscored by George too. 'I would like to speculate' Russel concludes, 'on the offspring of a marriage of (the) cultures, the Irish with the European, which cannot be kept apart for ever. There are intimations in the later poetry and prose of Yeats what an exciting literature might be born from that union.

George Russell sensed it prophetically, for Yeats was able to impart a dancing rhythm to his poetry. He could arrive at this easy felicity with wisdom because he could assimilate diverse strains of experiences of different cultures and their peoples from Ireland, England, Europe, India and other far-eastern countries. To get at the sub-stratum of human civilization, he studied with seriousness myths and legends of the past, with poetic insight; he incorporated these myths in his poems.

(iii) **Myths: Irish and others:** In the making of Yeats as a great poet, myths have played a great role. He drew much from the Celtic myths. One of them relates to the legendary hero, Finn (Find, Fionn, Fingal – different versions of Finn). He is a hero of the Ossianic or Fennian cycle of legends, supposed to have lived in the 3rd century Not only was he the leader of a band of warriors called fenians, but he was also the father of Ossian (or Oisin).

Oisin bridged the gap between the heroic pagan age and Irish Christianity. He is believed to have enjoyed longevity by virtue of his having a long sojourn in Fairyland. This legendary story evoked a dreak-like fantasy for Yeats. Precisely, he composed a narrative, the wanderings of Oisin with warmth and understanding. Specially, the closing lines of this poem reveal a characteristically Irish treatment of a traditional Irish theme:

Oisin Ah me! to be shaken with coughing and
broken with old age and pain,
Without laughter, a show unto children,
along with remembrance and fear;
All emptied of purple hours as a beggars
cloak in the rain,

As a hay-cock out on the flood, or a wolf
sucked under a weir.
It were said to gaze on the blessed and no
man I loved of old there;
I throw down the chain of small stones!
When life in my body has ceased,
I will go to Caoilte, and Conan,Bran,
Sceolan, Lomair,
And dwell in the house of the Fenians, be
they in flames or at feast.

Thematically, **The wanderings of Oisin** is opt an internalized quest-romance; it is an Irish poem, derived from two Gaelic sources, **Oicin i dtir na nog** and **Agallamh na senorach,** about a voyage to the heaven world. Not to get involved in scholastic heir-splitting as to whether the Oisin poem of Yeats, is a projection of Anglo-Irish mythological poetry or it is expressive of Irish spirit derived from its myths and legends, the point is that the poem is, in essence, 'a tissue of interlocked images.

Yeats, as he was emotively involved in Ireland's antiquity and its mythic images, he was equally interested in Indian myths and legends. In the poem, Yeats 'meru' avails the benefit of Indian symi.ols and myths to pass on the message of history in cosmic terms:

Civilization is hooped together, brought Under a rule, under the semblance of peace By manifold illusion; cut man's life is thought, And he, despite his terror, cannot cease Ravening through century after century, Ravening, raging, and uprooting that he may come Into the desolation of reality: Egypt and Greece, good-bye, and good-bye Rome ! Hermits upon Mount Meru or Everest, Caverned in night under the drifted snow, Or where that snow in winter's dreadful blast Beat down upon their naked bodies, know That day brings round the night, that before dawn His glory and his monuments are gone.

Yeats's search for mythic symbols going as far as to Indian antiquity stemmed from his intense desire not only to satisfy his soul's urgings cut also to convey through his poetry something from occultism and remote dimension.

(iv) **Occultism:** It constituted one of the major influences on Yeats's thinking and poetry. The influence of Madame Blavatsky and George Russell (AE) in terms of occultism and mysticism is quite well-known. However, if occult practices are considered as the main yardstick, the association of W.B.Yeats with W.T. Horton (1364-1919) is no less significant. Yeats maintained an occult friendship between them from 1896 to 1919. In fact, Yeats wrote 'A vision' under the deed and powerful influence of Horton. The way in which 'A Vision' was organised was 'said to develop ascrap by Horton.'

Yeats had a very illuminating and close friendship with Horton, though they had a great difference of opinion about sexual abstinence in terms of the occult practices expected of the members associated with the Hermetic Order of the Golden Dawn. Horton laid much importance on the sexual abstinence, but Yeats had his own reservations about it. Yeats had arrayed a different viewpoint to that of Horton in his philosophical essay, 'A vision' (1925), but still, he wanted to dedicate it to Horton: "le was my dear friend.... had he lived, I would have asked him to accept the dedication of a book I could not expect him (to) approve, he cared for little but what seemed to him a very simple piety.'

Having learned from slake that 'Opposition is true Friendship', Yeats never ceased to value the friendship of his strange but mighty opposite who warned him repeatedly to 'conquer & subordinate the dark horse to the white one': 'live the life & follow after Christ' ,he wrote when death was imminent; 'all else is delusion & Dead Sea fruit. ' Yeats in an introduction. to **A Book of Images,** published in 1898, containing a collection of Horton's drawings wrote that Horton "has his waking dreams and copies them in his drawings as if they were models posed for him by some earthy master. .... Even the phantastic landscapes, the entangled chimneys against a white sky, the dark valley with its little points of light, the cloudy and fragile towns and churches, are part of the history of a soul and whenever spiritual purpose mixes with artistic purpose, and not to its injury, it gives it a new sincerity, a new simplicity.'

'A Vision' , in Yeast's words, 'contains the epitome of the philosophy of human life which has occupied me for the last twenty years and will occupy me till I die. When these words were written, he had known Horton for more than twenty years.

(v) European Mystics: As part of Yeatsian Odyssey to know more and more of the deeper self of man, he also conducted numerous occult experiments with symbols; in this pursuit, he came to realize that 'image called up image in an endless procession.' He had earlier delved in a deeper Study of Irish folklore and mystic tradition out of his deeply felt urges to find intellectual justification for his Irish patriotism, and also to make his art a powerful vehicle for the benefit of his readers and Irish contem-poraries. Besides enriching his poetry, Yeats's purpose in discovering myths and symbols of different countries was to find out newer areas of subjective reality.

I had an unshakeable conviction arising how or whence I cannot tell, that invisible gates would open as they opened for Blake, as they opened for Swedenborg, as they opened for Boehme, and that this philosophy would find its manuals of devotion in all imaginative literature, and set before Irishmen for special manual an Irish literature, which, though made by many minds, would seem the work of a single mind, and turn our places of beauty or legendary association into holy symbols.

In the ninetees of the last century, Yeats was seized up with the Irish cause. In fact, at this period, he made vain attempts to create the ceremonies of an Irish Mystical order. It is in this context, he wanted to establish 'mysteries like those of Eleusis and Samothrace'. In his search for materials from which the ritual could be built for the order, he 'plunged without a clue into a labyrinth of images'. Obviously, this had a lasting and decisive effect on his later art. In a letter to Surge Moore, he observed: 'I always feel my work is not drama but the ritual of a lost faith.

Yeats's involvement in occultism, mysticism, folklore and various esoteric pursuits was actuated, apart from the compulsions of his art, to find true faith. It is in this respect he laboured hard to range his mental efforts in as diverse a field as he could do within his resources. Being an intensely Irish and conscious of his indebtedness to European civilisations, Yeats in his wider search for time-defying human traditions, he is not indifferent to the particular contribution of India in the context of the cultural progress of mankind.

Indifferent to history, India delighted in vast periods, which solemnized the mind, seeming to unite it to the ageless heavens. The Indian would have understood the dialectic of Balzac, but not that of Hegel – what could he have made of Hegel's optimism? – but never cared to discover in those great periods a conflict of civilisations and of nations.

This appraisal of India by Yeats may not appeal to modern Historians, but it does indicate the fact that Yeats understood the Indian viewpoint. He was liberal enough to understand the processes of history in a broader perspective. 'The historian thinks of Greece as an advance on Persia, of Rome as in something or other an advance on Greece, and thinks it impossible that any man could prefer the hunter's age to the agricultural. I, upon the other hand, must think all civilisations equal at their best: every phase returns, therefore in some sense every civilisation.

On going through this quotation, one thing that immediately strikes is that Yeats had a catholicity of mind. His view of human civilisation was visionary rather than analytic geared to the study of only concrete situations. His is a philosophical approach to the cultural history of man – which is essentially an Indian point of view:

Empty eyeballs knew
That knowledge increases unreality, that
Mirror on mirror mirrored is all the show.

These lines from his poem, 'The Statues' subsume the timeless wisdom of the East and specially that of India.

Yeats also attributes to Shakespeare the relevance of this approach towards terrestrial life in terms of Richard II in which the reigning King allows himself to be usurped by Bolingbroke, his cousin, partly on account of his philosophical indifference to the throne: ' He meditated as Solomon, not as Bentham meditated, upon blind ambitions, untoward accidents, and capricious passions, and the world was almost empty in his eyes as it much be in the eyes of God.' Here, Yeats has made an interesting analogy with Shakespeare's Richard II, for as he has made it clear in 'A Vision' referred to in the fore-going, for historical events do not take place mechanically.

(vii) **Nietzsche and French Symbolists:** Yeats had a great fascination for Nietzsche and French symbolists .By 1901-end, Yeats had developed fascination for Nietzsche; that strong enchanter, as he called him in a letter to Lady Gregory: 'Nietzsche completes Blake and has the same roots — I have not read anything with so much excitement since I got to love Morris's stories which have the same curious astringent joy.' His letters to George Russell (AE) on 14th May 1903 and to Quinn the next day are on Nietzsche. To Quinn, he wrote: 'I have always felt that the soul, has two movements primarily: one to transcend forms, and the other to create forms. Nietzsche calls these the Dionysian and Apollonic, respectively I think I have to some extent got weary of that wild God Dionysus, and I am hoping that the Far-Darter will come in his place.'Nietzsche has propounded that the interplay of Dionysian and Appolonian tendencies are necessary for the flowering of creativity in man. Yeats at one stage said: 'All civilization is held together by a series of suggestions made by an invisible hypnotist, artificially created illusions.' This notion is similar to the one answered by Nietzsche to his essay 'On Truth and lie in an Extra-Moral Sense'. According to Nietzsche, truth is 'a moving army of metaphors, metonymies, and anthropomorphisms, in short a summa of human relationships that are being poetically and rhetorically sublimated, transposed and beautified until, after long and repeated use, a people considers them as solid, canonical, and unavoidable. Truths are illusions whose illusionary nature has been forgotten.' There are various layers of influence of Nietzsche on Yeats.

Similarly, W.B. Yeats was greatly influenced by French symbolists in terms of aesthetics and style of poetry. The French symbolists were introduced to Yeats through Arthur Symon's book: **The Symbolist movement in Literature,** which was dedicated to W.B. Yeats because Yeats's approach to literature was largely symbolic. Of his debt towards Symons, Yeats was perfectly aware: 'my thoughts gained in richness and in clearness from his (Symon's) sympathy. 'Yeats considered Villiers' play Axel as a sacred book he longed for.There is an identity of life-circumstances specially in the early phase of their lives. Villiers was oration, belonging to a family of sailors and priests like Yeats's. He spent a dreamy youth on the beaches and the wild Mors. Yeats also took long walks on the shores near Sligo and listened to the fisherman's tales. Like Yeats, Villiers was fond of artistic literary milieus and the esoteric circles. "Villiers appears to John Charpentier as 'the". Very expression of the renaissance of the Celtic soul'". Above all, both had a liking for natural aristocracy. Yeats's prose – **Rosa Alchemica, The Tables of the** and **The Adoration of the Magi** and his drama, **The Shadowy waters** show influence of Villiers .One can make reference to numerous quotations from the writings of Villiers and Yeats which exhibit in a telling manner a great similarity of thought and feeling texture. For Yeats as well as for other symbolists the aesthetic mood mattered most. Their pursuit of beauty was essentially a religious approach to life and reality. In a paragraph later omitted from 'Rosa Alchemica', he traced the history of

that mood which Edgar Foe found in a wine-shop, and how it passed into France and took possession of Baudlaire, and from Baudlaire passed to England and the Pre-Raphaelites, and then again returned to France, and still wanders the world enlarging its power as it goes, awaiting the time when it shall be, perhaps, alone, or, with other moods, master over a great new religion, and an awakener of the fanatical wars that hovered in the gray surges, and forget the wine-cup where it was born.

Yeats was interested in symbols for their immense suggestiveness. Since the French symbolists, notably Stephane Mallarme (1842-98) and Villiers de L'Isle-Adam (1838-1889). The artist is able to coalesce the experience of dream and reality for the intellectually sensitive readers.Lawrence's trenchant observation - symbols are organic units of consciousness with a life of their own, and you can never explain them away, because their value is dynamic, emotional, belonging to the sense-consciousness of the body and soul, and not simply mental.' — Is help-ful for understanding Yeats's fascination for symbols and the great artists of the nineteenth century France who expanded the frontiers of aesthetic reality by giving a boa}, and shape to dreams and fantasies.

(viii) **Wilde, Parnell and Swift**: As part of the various influences on Yeats, one just cannot ignore the writings and the personalities of Oscar Wilde (1956-1900), Dramatist, poet, novelist and essayist; Charles Stewart Parnell (1846-1891) and Jonathan swift (1667-1745), Prose satirist, Critic and Poet. Like Yeats, they were Irish; and each of them contributed to the building up of Irish image. Wilde, Parnell was the national political leader of Ireland? Wilde and swift were writers and thinkers; and almost unsurpassable in their respective fields. Yeats was greatly influenced by their personalities as also by their signal contribution to the world of letters. All These great men proud of Ireland, and being aristocratic in taste and feelings, they were much admired by Yeats. In fact he derived much from Wilde and Swift in terms of his artistic pursuits. Yeats was much struck by the personality as correspondent in a suit for divorce by capt O' Shea against his wife in 1890. For Yeats as the Irish patriot, Parnell was the 'uncrowned' king of Ireland, even when his career was ruined by people opposed to him. 'Like Wilde, Parnell was an aristocrat seemed heroically romantic to Yeats, Finally, Yeats Wise of Na artistic punctuate. Victimized by the ignoble, however, his love for Katharine seemed heroically romantic to Yeats, Finally, Yeats merged the 'Parnell' figure with his own whether asserting aristocratic pride or rejecting unworthy modern Ireland. Parnell's being passionate yet self- controlled attracted Yeats much and by a passage of time, his image had acquired the Hero's mask, to be used by Yeats his death in 1900. To him, he had become 'the heroic victim of bankers, school masters, clergymen, not the flawed artist, he had become a mythic in the sacred conflict with those who would destroy beauty because of their inability to appreciate it. Jonathan Swift's ceaseless fight against 'cant, baseness, injustice and oppression' through his simple, clear incisive prose impressed Yeats mush so much so that he tried to follow swift to make his prose clear, simple and unambiguous.

By way of concluding works in regard to the various influences on Yeast's versatile sensibility it may be observed that Yeats was also greatly influenced by few ladies close to him. Ibsen's plays brought to the fore the identity of new woman. As an artist Yeats was equally interested in the quickened moods and fantasies of women. Of the women who influenced Yeats in one way or another are Lady Augusto Gregory, Maud Gonne, Olivia Shakespeare and Florence Farr. Yeasts's Interest in the mystery of women and their intellectual and physical attraction is explainable in terms of the disenchantment he had from his early- phase pursuits for purity and spirituality.

CHAPTER - II

SYMBOLS AND MYTHS - A FRAMEWORK

Whet one takes a closer look at modern literature say, from 1880 onward, one finds that sensitive men of letters—poets, artists, novelists and critics were in search of a newer form of literary genre. Ostensibly, faced with the cultured crises, they wanted to give a freer expression to their disenchantment with the socio-cultural reality of the day. It is this disenchantment among men of deeper sensibility that led to the growth of symbolic poetry and drama in France. In England too, writers started taking interest in symbolism and the symbolic movement originating in France. In this respect Symons's The Symbolist Movement in Literature (1899) proved catalytic for the dissemination of ideas associated with symbolism.

The trend towards symbolism among writers arose out of recoil from naturalism and realism. In their world- outlook, mere scrapy account of reality on surface did not matter much. They sought something more appealing and absorbing to their mind within the wider canvas of reality. Tried to project reality from inside out without being out off from outside. The French novelist, Honore de Balazc (1799 - 1850) and the Norwegian dramatist, Henrik Ibsen, (1828-1906) are by far the two outstanding men of 'a retreat' an internal distantiation from the very ideology from which their novels (and dramas) emerged. They make us 'perceive' (but not know) in some sense from the inside, by an internal distance, the very ideology in which they are held.

Men of literature were in search of new genres for realism had outlived its utility at least in terms of naturalisatistic style. Writers found themselves lost in the welter of confusion in the closing phase of Nineteenth century. Pre-Raphaelitism and latter Aestheticism were the offshoots of artists' reaction to the dismal profile of things in the latter half of the nineteenth century. W.B.Yeats was also familiar with Pre-Raphaelitism and Aestheticism (or the Art for Art's Sake that first originated in France and later in England). However, symbolism exercised a more powerful spell on his visionary from of mind.

With this introductory background in mind, it is now worthwhile to refer to Yeast's interest in symbols, myths, folklore and occultism. Yeats has availed not only myths and symbols but has also tried to introduce the spirit of symbolism and mythology in his poetry and dramas. However, before highlighting the relevant text from his poetry, it would be appropriate to touch upon the definitive terms relation to symbol and myth. Let us first take 'Symbol' which is defined, straightforwardly by Kant (who, in his Critique of Judgments, 1790, calls it an 'aesthetic idea) in terms of the 'attributes of an object' which serve the rational idea as a substitute for logical presentation. (But more than this the proper function a symbol is to animate) the mind by opening out.... kindred representations stretching beyond its 'Ken' (his examples are the eagle that stands for Jove and the peacock that represents Juno) takes on a spatial significance for Romantics early (Coleridge) and late (Yeasts). Yeats indeed goes so far as to maintain that 'a continuous indefininable symbolism' is 'the substance of all style (The symbolism of Poetry, 1900). And for him the excellence of a symbol consists in the suggestiveness that derives from the suppression 'as a sword-blade may flicker with light of burning towers' so the symbols evoke the unseen worlds.

In the same way, to get a proper grasp of Yeats's poetry, one should know the definitive connotation o myth. it is closely related to symbol. According to D.H. Lawrence 'the images of myth are symbols. They don't 'mean something. They stand for

Units of human feelings and experience is a symbol. And the power of the symbol is to arouse the deep emotional self, and the dynamic self, beyond comprehension. Many ages of accumulated experience still throbe within a symbol. And we throb in response. It takes Centuries to create a, really significant. Even the symbol of the Cross, or of the horse-shoe, or the horns. 'Underscoring the special significance of a symbol Lawrence has pointed out that a symbol just cannot be invented in one stride. It takes a long time and a combine action of forces involving men with deep sense of vision and sensibility.

W.B Yeats, as a 'poet of deep vision, was alive to the immense potentialities of myths and symbols. .That is why; he got himself deeply interested in understanding not only Irish myths and folkloric tales and symbols, but also those of other countries. 'From Swedenborg and William, villagers de L'Ist e-Adam, and Maeterlinck, he derived the view of poetry as a relation of the invisible in a complex figurative language. Yeats's drama, like his poetry, reflects his effort to wed the aristocratic and highly conceptualized art of the symbolists to the legendary and mystical traditions of the Irish history, legend or popular superstitions of the Irish folk.

Yeats was drawn to symbolism and mythology because through the use of symbols and myths he wanted to unravel the mystery of life. Yeats availed the symbolic and mythic expression in his poetry and drama for suggestive and evocative purposes. In this way, he tried to present the mystery of being through the transcendence of the finite. In some of his poetic expressions, one comes across the veritable life-continuum in all its density and complexity. For example, as one goes through the third stanza, of his poem Blood and the /moon. 11 one feels as if Yeats, who had been greatly shocked by the foul murder of the Irish Free State Government, was trying to web out different strands of his mind, agog – in a state of reverie from different image such as 'moon', blood of innocence' ancestral stair' with 'odour of blood, 'drunken frenzy' and the bid at the 'purity of the unclouded moon'. Even with some shades of obscurity this stanza may be quoted here.

The purity of the unclouded moon
Has flung its arrowy shaft upon the floor.
Seven centuries have passed and it is pure
The blood of Innocence has left no stain.
There, on blood-saturated, have stood
Soldier, assassin, executioner,
Whether for daily pittance or In blind feat
Or out of abstract hatred, and shed blood,
But could not cast a signal jet thereon.
Odour of blood on the ancestral stair.
And we that have shed none must gather there
And clamour in drunken frenzy for the moon.

Some of the symbolism of this poem was suggested by the waste room at the top of Thoor ballylee, where butterflies entered by the loopholes and died against the window-panes. Yeats Selected pansy (Macmillan 1969)

The Coellected poems of W.B.Yeats, (Macmillan, 1952)

W.B.Yeats, as a poet of deep vision, was alive to the immense potentities

In these lines. Sound and sense gets fused; and as a result, the poet is able to project a segment of 'feeling-and-thought' pattern that he experiences of myths and symbols. That is way, he got himself deeply interested in understanding not only Irish myths and folkloric tales and symbols, but also those of other contries. 'Fro Swedenborg and William Balke as well as from Mallarme, villagers de L'Isie-Adam, and Materlinck, he derived the view of poetry as a relation of the invisible in a complex figurative Language. Yeats's drama, like his poetry, reflects his effort to wed the aristocratic and highly conceptualized are of the symbolists to the legendary and mystical traditions of the Irish history, legend r popular superstitions of the Irish folk.'

Yeats was drawn to symbolism and mythology because through the use of symbols and myths he wanted to unravel the mystery of life. Yeats availed the symbolic and mythic expression on his poetry and symbolic and mythic expression in his poetry and dream for suggestive and evocative purposes. In this way, he tried to present the mystery of being through the transcendence of the finite. In some of his poetic expressions, one comes across the veritable life -continuum in all its

Through the etymological Interpretation of symbol has shown Its vast potentiality for depicting life in a deeper perspective. Writing to his father, 5 March 1916. Yeats underscored this 'standpoint:

You spoke of all art as imitation, meaning, I conclude, imitation of something in the other world. To me it seems that it often uses the outer world as a symbolism to express subjective moods. The greater the subjectivity , the less limitation The element of pattern in every art, is I think, the part that is not imitative, for in the last analysis there will always be somewhere an intensity of pattern that we have never seen with our eyes. In fact, imitation seems to me to create a language in which we say things which are not imitation.

For Yeats' art provided occasion for transcending empirical reality.. As already touched upon in first chapter, Yeats from his early childhood was receptive to diverse influences, such as folklore ,myths, symbols - Irish and others, mysticism and occult experiences.. Moreover, he was also a staunch Irish patriot. Further, besides understanding poetic tradition, especially of the west (though it is true he was also interested in Japanese Noh plays), Yeats was also interested in novel, as an art form. These diverse influences made his poetry rich and at the same time quite suggestive. Apparently, he developed sufficient flair to appreciate the intuitive potency of symbols myths, and above all in using them to immense poetic advantage. Yeats's poetry .is also enriched by his using the literary device of 'Persona' it helped him to objectify his subjective feelings on various aspects of life and reality. For example, the lines

There in the tomb stand the dead upright,
But winds come up from the shore;
They shake when the winds roar,
Old bones upon the mountain shake.

In the poem 'The Black Tower' are suggestive of a tragic mood built up out of the bones of a megalithic warrior interred in a tomb near Sligo (Ireland).

Yeats's imagination imparts historicity to the imagined 'Black Tower' by linking it with a tomb near Sligo in which the bones of the warrior were found. Yeats introduces a human factor in this poem in the next stanza:

Those banners come to bribe or threaten
Or whisper that a man's a fool
Who, when his own right king's forgotten,
Cares what king sets up his rule.

This is generally the case. Kings either out of haughtiness or self-complacency forget the devotion of their loyal subjects. In the same token, a reference to the tower's old cook (penultimate stanza) about the telling a lie that 'he hears the king's great born' put a mask of reality to the imagined tower. The image of the faint moonlight' and 'the dark grows blacker' over the tomb in the second and third 4-lines stanza imply that the cycle of nature has its own say about the bones of a megalithic warrior interred in a tomb.

To show the importance of Yeats as a poet of deep insight and power, a slight digression is necessary to be aware of the crucial importance of language for poetry. 'The poetic use of language is distinguished from other uses through the fact that, in poetry, language is perceived in itself and not as a transparent and transitive of "something else". Poetic language is autotelic language. The expression 'autotelic' implies the idea of 'being an end in itself ; and this comes to take place when a poet is able to avail the creative potentialities of mythic and symbolic language—either by drawing upon the existing myths and symbols, or through the self Objectivities of one's inmost feelings, as Yeatss does in a number of his poems.

If one takes a close look at 'Under .Ben Bulben', one finds that by fusing disparate elements of thought reality, he is able to make a lasting impression on the mind of a reader whereby he is able to think in deeper terms on life, destiny and death. He penned a hieratic mode of poetry to find out a way of ascension amidst the modern complexity. His poetry is his own autobiography set in language which is both symbolic and mythical. 'Under Ben Bulben' is considered Yeats's own epitaph and elegy has a startling twelve-line stanza of which the first six lines may be quoted to show that this great poet refferred to myths and symbols from earlier poetry. In doing so, he was able to make a ponderous effect.

Swear by what the sages spoke
Round the Mareotic Lake
That the Witch of Atlas knew,
Spoke and set the cocks a-crow

Swear by those: horsemen, by those women
Complexion and form prove superhuman, 20

It reminds us something of the metaphysical frenzy Macbeth might have felt on encountering the three witches in the beginning of Shakespeare's play.

What is striking is the insistent urgency with which Yeats prepares his epitaph.

In the second stanza, Yeats has lent a mythic

Coloring to facts of history and human reality

Many times man lives and dies
Between his two eternities,
That of race and that of soul,
And of ancient Ireland knew it all.
Whether man die in his bed
the rifle knocks him dead,
A brief parting from those dear
Is the worst man has to fear.
Though grave-diggers' toil is long,
Sharp their spades, their muscles strong
They but thrust their buried men
Back in the human mind again.[21]

Here, Yeats expresses his concern with life and destiny as a man from Ireland; and not as a sophisticated intellectual. There is an epiphanic concern with life, death, graveyard and their impact on human sensibility. It is the feeling of an Irish peasant not cut off from the folklore ways of looking at reality. In country Sligo he discovered the map of the territory of his own its contours in hill and wood, wind and weather, bird and beast.

Yeats himself has acknowledged it. 'I have been at no pains to separate my own beliefs from those of the Peasantry, but have rather let man and woman, dhouls and fearies, go their way unoffended or defended by any argument of mine. The things a man has heard and seen 23 are the threads of life.' The rider falls on 'the threads of life'. He has composed 'under Ben Bulbun' with this awareness. The expression 'Though grave-diggers toil is long they but thrust their buried men. is essentially folklorist, for it is the cemetery or grave-yard that reminds living men not only about the transiency of life but also about the passing away of the loving ones. Thus Yeats is able to evoke the continuity of life and the inter-relationship of men and women across a long stretch of time originating in myth and legend.

The entire fourth stanza of 'Under Ben Bulben' is full of meaning. It carries an abiding message. The first five lines

Poet and sculptor, do the work,
Nor let the modish painter shirk
What his great forefathers did,
Bring the soul of man to God,
Make him fill the cradles right --

remind readers to note that it is the creative artists that give direction to man, born unregenerate as he is.

In the second part of this stanza, the four lines –

Michael Angelo left a proof
On the Sistine Chapter roof,
Where but half-awakened Adam
Can disturb globe-trotting Madam –

Yeats conveys the experiential homely truth that mind, which is as yet unprepared to appreciate the spiritual meaning of art and the belief in God as it is the case with an American woman on a sight-seeing in hurry. The moral is that the unregenerate mind of human beings in chaotic conditions of modern life blasphems anything which is beautiful and carries a divine spark in it. Michelangelo, the famous artist from Italian renaissance whose paintings on walls and ceilings of Sistine Chapel have a mark of perfectibility; and the art-feelings that he projects is to remind man of the magnificence of God and Divine Life. This is what is conveyed by Yeats in the concluding lines of the fourth stanza: '.Quattrocento put in paint / on backgrounds for a God or Saint / That heavens had opened.'

The last stanza of 'Under Ben bulben' is an in vocation is an invocation to the Irish spirit and a stirring appeal to Irish poets to be true to humanity of Ireland, and not to get reconciled as Base-born products of base beds.' This stanza is significant in our understanding Yeats's metaphysical attachment to Ireland and Irish spirit. when Yeats, the poet in the making, develops awareness of the plight of his people, in the closing phase of the nineteenth century he gets involved culturally and politically in the destiny of Ireland....' ... for an Irish poet there was at that time little to build on. There was the oral tradition of the Irish poor, and an ancient literature written in a language now spoken only by largely illiterate class; and there was a totally unrelated Anglo-Irish culture belonging to Yeats's own class, the Protestant ascendancy, whose great names, Burke and Grattan, Swift and Goldsmith and Berkeley were unknown to the Gaelic tradition. In Four Years (1887-1891) Yeats tell how he had realized that he must build a new tradition.'

It is in this background if one goes through the lines: 'Irish poets, learn your trade, / Sing whatever is well made That we in coming days may be / still the indomitable Irishry' in the fifth stanza, one comes to realize the eytent of Yeats's involvement in Irish resurgence. The most remarkable point is that he did not want to anglify Irish culture but to 're-present' the ancient glory of Ireland run down of late in terms of interpreting the rich oral, folkloric tradition through the medium of modern poetry rendered in English. Yeats himself acknowledged it: 'There was no help for it, seeding that my country was not born at all' 31in modern sense. It would not be out of context to comment that Yeats in remembering Ireland with all the feelings of sacredness was an actor and martyr to the Irish cause. Precisely, he touched upon this cherished subject in the closing days of his life, and in doing so, he has left behind an Irish myth of 'the indomitable Irishry'. 'Under Ben Bulben's last six lines

"No marble, no conventional phrase;
On limestone quarried near the spot
By his command these words are cut:
Cast a cold eye
On life, on death.
Horseman, pase by

which constitute the actual epitaph needs to be treated hermeneutically. In these words, Yeats the poet is duly mythologized in terms that are truly mythical and full of ·grandeur. Both Ezra Found (1835-1 72) and T.5. Eliot (1888-1.965) have eulogized the concept woven around 'the impersonality of an artist': and in this respect, W.B.Yeats: acquits amply well. Myth-oriented as his mind is, Yeats takes an impersonal view of life and death. His poser is why one (who is close to the poet) should shed sentimental tears. Death and life are part of the cosmic circuit; and the true wisdom lies in accepting it as it is. T'hat is why Yeats says : 'Horseman, pass by! Don't linger in tears. This imparts a symbolic gravity to Yeats's life.

"In an essay on 'Ireland and the Arts', Yeats recalls a time when he was 'without any decided impulse to one thing more than another, and especially to those who are convinced, as I was convinced, that art is tribeless, nationless, a blossom gathered in No Man's land.' ....'when I first wrote I went here and there for my subjects as my reading led me, and preferred to all other countries Arcadia and the India of romance, but presently I convinced myself for such reasons as those in Ireland and the Arts, that I should never go for the scenery of a poem to any country but my own, and I think that I shall hold that conviction to the end. It remained a life-long resolution with him. Ireland became a great symbol of his life which beckoned to him from one stage to another. In point of reality;;, his Ireland. Was more than the Ireland of history? Imaginatively, he viewed Ireland with mythic solemnity. In his writings, he is felicitous about the subject of Ireland, its people and the peculiar 'Irish' way of looking at the reality he encapsulated in his mind as and when he came across 'the poor and dispossessed and illiterate' folk of Ireland, listening to their untarnished stories. His essay, 'Ireland and the Arts' shows the indebtedness of Yeats to his country:

> **The Greeks, the only perfect artists of the world, looked within their own borders, and we, like them, have a history fuller than in any modern history of imaginative events; and legends which surpass, as I think, all legends but theirs in wild beauty, and in our land, as in theirs, there is no river or mountain that is not associated in the memory with some event or legend....I would have Ireland recreate the ancient arts, the arts as they were understood in Judaca, in India, in Scandinavia, in Greece and Rome, in every ancient land; as they were understood when they moved a whole people and not a few people who have grown up in a leisured class and made this understanding their business.**

The rocky terrain of Ireland with its peculiar wilderness sustained Yeats much in his search for symbols and myth. He put a question straightaway: 'Have not all races had their first unity from a mythology that marries them to rock and hills? He looked with powerful imagination to the day when Ireland would be great. He wanted to create the Irish Myth; and in this direction, he wanted to 'deepen the political passion of the nation, that all, artist and poet, craftsman and day-labourer would accept a common design' so that 'Perhaps even those images, once created and associated with river and mountain, might have of themselves and with some powerful, even turbulent life.'

In dilating upon symbols and myths in Yeats's poetry, his views on having 'Mask' about himself. He attached a great value to it in the sense that by wearing a mask – connated by thoughts and feelings wallowing within one's deep unconscious, one is able to have 'The Anti-Self' – to use the Yeatsian expression (which connote the notion of 'alter ego' or second self in simpler language); and then, as Yeats has shown in his poem 'Ego Dominus Thus' the tense dialectic whereby the poet is able to arrive at a metaphysical grasp of conflicts and tensions standing in the way of one's realizing true self. Yeats did not want to be deluged by subjective feelings alone; he wanted to avail the full potential of possibilities out of the dynamic harmonisation of objectivity and subjectivity. His own reasoning accords with this interpretation:

> Some years ago I began to believe that our culture,
> with its doctrine of sincerity and self-realisation,
> made us gentle and passive, and that the Middle Ages
> and the Renaissance were right to found theirs upon
> the imitation of Christ or of some classic hero.
> St Francis and Caesar Borgia made themselves over-
> mastering, creative persons by turning from the
> mirror to meditation upon a mask.

The wearing of mask comes out of one's awareness to give a shape and location to the bubbling reveries with-in oneself. Yeats as an artist did not want to remain deluded by mere sentiments. 'Hence, he argues the need for building an antithetical self:

> **Nor has any poet I have read of or heard or met**
> **with been a sentimentalist. The other self, the**
> **anti-self or the antithetical self, as one may**
> **choose to name it, comes but to those who are no**
> **longer deceived, whose passion is reality. The**
> **sentimentalists are practical men who believe in**
> **money, in position, in a marriage bell, and whose**
> **understanding of happiness is to be so busy whether**
> **at work or play, that all is forgotten but the**

> **momentary aim. They find their pleasure in a cup that is filled from Lethe's wharf, and for the awakening, for the vision, for the revelation of reality, tradition offers us a different word — ecstasy.**

This is defence of a true poet in eloquent terms. To get bogged down either by objectivity or subjectivity is not very helpful to realise the impersonality of poetic self. "(Reality', for Yeats, is neither to be found in that buried self which directs and orders a man's life or in its mask, the anti-self, but in the product born of their struggle. Extroverts, Yeats felt, must flee their masks. Introverts -painters , writers, musicians, all creative men - must recognize their own proper masks. , ideal opposites, and in trying to become those nearly impossible other selves creat the dramatic tensions from which art arises. The doctrine of the mask erects, therefore , on the artist's personality a kind of private mythology in which the individual struggles to become that which is most unlike himself.....'

Yeats, being a creative artist, has to choose by necessity an interovert's mask—patterned on some hero or a man of action of the past.In terms of his interest in Ireland and Irish legends and myths, it was but natural that Yeats should imagine himself out in terms of Cuchulain,

- - a hero striding out of the remote legendary Irish past, a man of action, great fighter and great lover., Yeats justified that approach because he loved Ireland and its glory. In terms of his **alter ego** (Yeatsian term : 'anti-self) he tried to re-incarnate Cuchulain's Ireland; its heroes and their superhuman achievements :

We had in Ireland imaginative stories, which the uneducated classes knew and even sang, and might we no make those stores current among the educated classes, rediscovering for the work's sake what I have called 'the applied arts of literature, the association of literature, that is , with music, speech, and dance; and at last, it might be, so deepen the political passion of the nation that all, artist and poet, craftsman and day-labourer would accept a common design?

Here, a reference to his philosophical prose - work,

A vision towards which he was preparing mentally before his marriage with Miss Hyde-Lees on 20th October 1917 as he wrote to his father about his being deeply engaged in discovering a religious system more or less logically worked out. A system which will, I hope, interest you as a form of poetry. A find the setting of if all in order has helped my verse, has given me a new framework and new patterns. One goes on year after year getting the disorder of one's mind in order, and this is the real impulse to create.

His marriage hastened the finalisation of A Vision.

It was published in 1925, and it is considered as 'the culmination of Yeats's attempts to find something in which he could believe.' (A deeper study of A Vision would be made only in the fifth chapter; here a passing reference would be made to show its importance in terms of the application of 'masks' in his poetry. The most eloquent illustration of his theory of mask, one finds in his poem, 'Ego Domisnus Tuus' in dialogue from in which 'Hic' represents the empirical self while 'Ille' stands Yeats's alter ego (anti-self in his terminology). Through the verbal dielectric of Hic and Ille, one gets to know the opinion of Yeats on Keats as also on Dante. 'Hic' initiates the dialogue in an ironical manner:

Hic. .... A lamp burns on beside the open book That Michael Robartes left, you walk in the moon.

And, though you have passed the best of life, still trace.

Enthralled by the unconquerable delusion.

Magical shapes.

Ille By the help of an image

I call to my own opposite, summon all

That I have handled least, least looked upon.

Hic And I would find myself and not an image.

Ille That I sour modern hope, and by its light we have lit upon the gentle, sensitive mind And lost the old nonchalance of the hand; whether we have chosen chisel, pen or brush, we are but critics, or but half create, Timid, en tangled, empty and abashed, Lacking the countenance of our friends.

When 'Hic' observed that 'the chief imagination or Christendom' found expression through Dante Alighiert through his single-minded devotion and asceticism 'That he has made that hollow face of his / More plain to the mind's eye...', Ille' replied ironically - -

And did he find himself

Or was the hunger that had made it hollow A hunger for the apple on the bough Most out of reach ? and is that spectral image The man that Lapo and that Guido knew? I think he fashioned from his opposite An image that might have been a stony face Staring upon a Bedouin's horse-hair roof From doored and windowed cliff, or half upturned Among the coarse grass and the camel-dung. He set his chisel to the hardest stone.

The deep moral 'Ille' hammers home is that a true artist like Dante was able to get a vision of reality in spite of his having been derided by worldly people for 'his lecherous life'. 'And the divine image of Beatrice is a superior compensation for what had been lost in experience.,

To 'Hic's' pointer that John keats was able to arrive at arrive at expression without having to wader through a dissipated life, 'Ille' comments critically on John keats –

For certainly he sank into his grave
His senses and his heart unsatisfied
And made - - being poor, ailing and ignorant
Shut out from all the luxury of the world
That coarse-bred son of a livery-stable keeper - -
Luxuriant song .

It is a doctrinal commen on keats; but whatever it is, Yeats wanted to make it clear that womanly passion, as it is, has to be steered through to arrive at one's clear-cut certitude. It this respect, Byron's comment also holds true. One's ideals connoted in a mask of 'Anti-self' get fully crystallised while developing one's intellectual insight.

In the context of 'A Vision', that comment - - 'Passionate emotion is of particular importance to the poets of phase 17, Dante and Yeats among them. The mask of phase 17 which he calls the 'mask of simplicity' (A Vision) must be emotional to balance the increasing intellectuality and abstraction of the third quarter,' - - holds good.

By way of concluding assessment of 'Ego Dominus Tuus., as one ponders over 'Hic 's' remark : 'A style is found by sedentary toil / And by the imitation of great masters, one deciphers from 'Ille 's' reply, quoted below, Yeats actually aspired to be a master by his own artistic efforts. The only fear he has that he may not be 'blasphemed., - -

Because I seek an image, not a book.
Those men that in their writings are most wise
Own nothing but their blind, stupefied hearts.
I call to the mysterious one who yet
Shall walk the wet sands by the edge of the stream
And look most like me, being indeed my double,
And prove of all imaginable things
The most unlike, being my anti-self
And, standing by these characters, disclose
All that I seek; and whisper it as though
He were afraid the birds, who cry aloud
Their momentary cries before it is dawn.
Would carry it away to blasphemous men.

The complicated world of today in all its complexity gets 'entextured' in the poems of W.B. Yeats. His doctrine of 'anti-self' helps Yeats to encompass the opposing shores of reality without losing his geet on ground. In itself, it is a remarkable achievement. The last stanza of the third poem of 'Nineteen Hundred and Nineteen' - - 'The swan has leaped into the desolate heaven: — — /Learn that we were crack-pated when we dreamed,' has a bearing to the Irish Rebellion in 1916; and the way, Yeats reacts to the violent events get symbolised and then expressed in terms almost mythic. 'The passage embodies Yeats's' effort, in the civil-war sequences, to confront the murderous desolation he feels at the heart of modern existence and to find a stay against personal chaos.,

As part of the concluding remarks on this chapter, one may refer to a number of poems, such as 'Byzantium;

'The Black Tower,' 'Adam's Curse,' 'Sailing to Byzantium,'

'Crazy Jane' poems, 'The shadowy waters,' 'The wild sawans at coole,' 'Supernatural songs' poems and practically all the 'Last poems significant from the standpoint of an exposition of symbols and myths in Yeats's poetry. Yeats was also to do it because he took painstaking efforts to be conscientious and scrupulous in making his poems symbolic expressions of the poets, who was not only a skilled practitioner in versification, but was also a man of many parts - a man of vision, occult-practitioner, philosopher, Politician and above all a man of feelings with warmth and understanding. This element of versatility in his help to create poems of dancing rhythm carrying an aroma of holiness and mythic grandeur.

CHAPTER – III

SYMBOLS AND MYTHS FROM IRISH FOLKLORE

Irish folklore exercised an abiding impression on W.B. Yeats. In point of reality, as a poet, he drew much sustenance from time folklore traditions of not only Ireland but also of other countries. His close contact with Irish people and their joys and sorrows enabled him to develop into a poet with classical dignity. It saved him in many a way from 'Lachrymose' form of romanticism and desiccative sensibility.

> I no longer live an elaborate and haughty life,
> but seek to lose myself among the prayers and
> the sorrows of the multitude. I pray best in
> poor chapels, where frieze costs brush against
> me as I kneel, and when I pray against the
> demons I repeat a prayer which was made I know
> not how many centuries ago to help was made I know
> Gaelic man or woman who had suffered with a
> suffering like mine :
>
> Seven paters seventimes,
> Send Mary by her son,
> Send Bridget by her mantle,
> Send God by His strength,
> Between us and the faery host,
> Between us and the demons of the air.

Real men of flesh and blood, unlike the typefied petti-bourgeoies, experience the awful dangers from demons in one form or another; and then, in a state of agonized frame of mind, they prayfully appeal to God to save them from the agonized strife, within themselves.

The most important point that should be borne in mind here is that even though he had a **visionary frame of mind, yet he was drawn to common people in Ireland.**

Yeats's interest in Irish folklore dates back to his early childhood. In the 1880s, John O'Leary was the elder statesman of the Irish nationalism. Yeats came under his influence.

> Helped by O'Leary's books and encouragement, Yeats deepened his knowledge of Irish history and folklore, and while on visits to his uncle, George pollexfen, in sligo, he learned a great deal about the folklore of that area from his uncle's servant Mary Battle, who provided him with much of the material which he later collected in **The celtic Twilight.**

county sligo, the area to which Yeats's mother belonged, became an inspiring symbol to aid, off and on, the young Yeats to put into effect the dense texture of reality in his poetry. With impassioned feeling, he remembers the real and mythological territory of county sligo and its environs in his poem, 'Under Saturn':

Do not because this day I have grown saturnine Imagine that lost live, inseparable from my though Because I have no other youth, can make me pine; For how should I forget the wisdom that you brought, The comfort that you made? Although my wits have gone on a fantastic ride, my horse's flanks are spurred By childish memories of an old cross pollexfen, And of a Middleton, whose name you never heard, And of a red-haired Yeats whose looks, although he died Before my time, seem like a vivid memory.

You heard that labouring man who had served my people

He said

Upon the open road, near to the sligo quay –
No, no, not said, but cried it out – 'You have come again.
And surely after twenty years it was time to come.
I am thinking of a child's vow sworn in vain
Never to leave that valley his fathers called their home.

In this expressive poem, Yeats lays bare his indebtedness to Sligo, his elder family members from mother's side, not-too-known Middleton yet a man worthy of remembrance; and then, and ordinary labourer welcoming Yeats with deep feeling of love to remind that Yeats has unbreakable bonds with sligo and its warm-hearted people. By writing this poem, Yeats wants to tell his readers that his country-folk though practically unknown had human heart, the paucity of which makes men of intellection in urban pockete of metropolitan cities depressive and desiccative. It is in this background, Yeats understood the vital importance of the living touch of common people; and it is more so, in the revages of industrialisation at the time Yeats lived.

With his interest in Irish myths and his country's fight for political independence, he assigned a religious significance to Ireland's bid to assert itself. However, being given to visionary reveries from his early child- hood, he developed a 'monkish hate' against the Victorian science and social realism. He called the outlook associated with industrialism and Victorian profile of things harmful for the proper growth of human personality. He had a great satisfaction that Irish people were free from its baneful influence.

Because of his inborn penchant for mysticism, Yeats got himself involved in deciphering the myths and legends of Ireland. It also explains his love for loneliness and wisdom from his early childhood. 'But, even from George (his uncle, George Pollexfen), Willy (W. B. Yeats) did ambition – suggested by Thoreau's **Walden** – to live in a cottage on a little island in Lough Gill called innisfree. "Having conquered bodily desire and the inclination of the mind towards women and love", he had decided quite finally to life "seeking wisdom", For him the hidden should be made plain. Then in Slish wood he remained stark awake, all night, worrying about the wood ranger. At dawn Innisfree emerged from darkness, and he lay in ecstasy nothing the order of the cry of birds. The next day when he tried to explain an unimaginable sleepiness, a servant embarrassed him with insinuating fits of laughter. 'You had good right to be fatigued."

W. B. Yeats endeared himself to the common people because he remained responded to them in an open –

Hearted manner. His poems provide glimptain of his love for Irish people on deep, affirmative, philosophical dimension.

> A conscious mystic, now brother of vanished Druids,
> he had designs upon the whole of the supernatural.
> The apparitions seen by Sligo peasants — were they
> the ancient Irish gods? And how did these gods fit
> in with the religion taught in churches? His cousin
> Lucy Middleton described more strange happening
> at Ballisodare and Rosses; and he himself heard a
> sound as of peas thrown against a mirror, and now
> the earth under some trees blaze with light, and
> then a brilliant torch moving along the river, 'I kept
> asking myself if I could be deceived, 'when an eery
> light started to climb the cairn of knocknarea,
> he timed it. Five minutes to reach the top : Had human
> steps such speed? The supernatural engrossed him.
> Wandering about raths and faerie hills, he questioned
> old women and old men, and believed with his emotions.
> But he dreaded being called a fool, and "was always
> ready to deny or turn into a joke what was for all that
> my secret fanaticism,"

He remained true to his daemon even at the risk of his being misunderstood. He continued to draw sustenance from Ireland and its people. It was his destiny to know more and more about

Irish spirit, which he found healing as also revealing. This is what one gets out of his poem: 'Into the Twilight':

> Out-worn heart, in a time out-worn,
> Come clear of the nets of wrong and right;
> Laugh, heart, again in the grey twilight;
> Sigh, heart, again in the dew of the morn.
> Your mother Eire is always young,
> Dew ever shining and twilight grey;
> Though hope fall from you and love decay
> Burining in fires of a slanderous tongue.
> Come, heart, where hill is heaped upon hill :
> For there the mystical brotherhood
> of sun and moonand hollow and wood
> And river and stream work out their will.

Here, nature is celebrated with pagan enthusiasm.

For Yeats, the chief religious concern was to live up to his personal religion as he discovered in the course of his encounter with the my theology of Irish folkore and the occlt, as well as in resolving the various problems: autobiographical and political. In this context, one can refer to the III section of his poem, 'The Tower', He celebrates man's freedom in its crystalline affirmative stance. The man of honour who stand by their uptrightness in the thick of life's struggle. In an impassioned mood, he says : 'It is time that I wrote my will : / I choose upstanding men / That climb the streams until / The fountain leap, and at dawn / Drop their cast at the side / of dripping stone; I declare / The pride of people that were / Bound neither to cause nor to state, / Neither to slaves that were spat on, / Nor to the tyrants that spat, / That people of Burke and of Grattan / That gave, though free to refuse - / Pride, like that of the morn, … …. or that of the hour / when the swan must fix his eye / Upon a fading gleam, / Float out upon a long / last reach of glittering stream / And there sing his last song ,'

And then, by way of conclusion, Yeats remarks about the desirability of affirming one's destiny without forsaking the basic life - issue :

> And I declare my faith :
> I mock Plotinus' through
> And cry in Plato's teeth,
> Death and life were not
> Till man made up the whole,
> Made lock, stock and barrel
> Out of his bitter soul,
> Aye, sun and moon and star, all,
> And further add to that
> That, being dead, we rise,
> Dream and so create
> Translunar Paradise.
> I have prepared my peace
> with learned Italian things
> And the proud stones of Greece,
> Poet's imaginings
> And memories of love,
> Memories of the words of women,
> All those things whereof
> Man makes a superhuman
> Mirror-r-resembling dream.

For Yeats, life celebrates its triumph when the person concerned is aware of the multi-dimentionality of reality in which dream and substance play their due role.

Intre - celluler weave of life is extremely complex; and Yeats, as a poet interested in myths and symbols, both dating to the remote period of history and to those which are contemporaneous bring them into focus. In the line under under reference, one can get a feeling that Yeats was not only influenced by the folk-spirit of Ireland, but also by Shakespeare and the German philosopher, Friederich Nietsche (1844 – 1900). In terms of dramatic intensity, there is an affinity to Nietzsche's figure for the 'genius in the act of creation,,,,,, (can create) the weird image ...... is at once subject and object, at once poet, actor and spectator,'

Like Nietzsche, Yeats held that nothing is to be avoided, one must have the grit of character to transmute even lust and rage, as can be learned from Yeats's 'The Spurt

> You think it horrible that lust and rage
> Should dance attendance upon my old age;
> They were not such a plague when I was young;
> What else have I to spur me into a song ?

Yeats had also a penetrating eye on the contemporaneous events. His quatrain : 'The Great Day' is revealing enough to show that Yeats understood the purport of revolutionary politics of his time and it is relevant of revolutionary politics of his time and it is relevant even today. The poet who was steeped in folk-lore knew that basic life issue just cannot be resolved at the political level :

> Hurrah for revolution and more cannon shot ;
> A beggar upon horseback lashes a beggar upon foot;
> Hurrah for revolution and cannon come again,
> The beggars have changed places but the lash goes on.

The message is clear enough. One ruling despotism changes into another. So, common people should take into account this aspect of reality and should not fritter away their life-span over the ideal of social change which goes chimerical in the ultimate analysis. Through his writings, Yeats cautioned Irish people against going for swift-moving social changes, externally manipulated. He did no want them to become **deracine** by cutting themselves from the traditional values sustained on a wide net-work of oral legends and folk-myths. It is equally true to say that his involvement with the joys and sorrows of his people was responsible for his interest in Irish folklore and mythology.

The overall message of Yeats's poetry and other writings is that man belittles his life through non-symbolic mode of existence in which the chief criterion is that of money and its value-system. Poem after poem, Yeats reminds his country to develop a taste for time eternal values of life. For example, in a poem, 'A Faery song, ' Yeats appeals to all those who are old and who have not lost the sense of gaiety should bear in mind to

Give to these children, new from the world,
Silence and love;
And the long dew-dropping hours of the night,
And the stars above ;

as well as 'Rest far from men'. similarly, the first stanza of the poem, 'When you are old 'Carries a striking piece of wisdom:

When you are old and grey and full of sleep,
And nodding by the fire, take down this book,
And slowly read, and dream of the soft look
Your eyes had once, and of their shadows deep.

The second stanza of this poem is equally meaningful and is an unbeguiled study of man's short sojourn on this planet, his quest for the unknown and his involvement in unavoidable sorrows. The poem, 'who goes with Fergus?' is based upon the Irish legend and is exhortatory in spirit;

Who will go drive with Fergus now,
And pierce the deep wood's woven shade,
Young man, lift up your russet brow,
And lift your tender eyelids, maid,
And brood on hopes and fear no more.
And no more turn aside and brood
Upon love's bitter mystery;
For Fergus rules the brazen care,
And rules the shadows of the wood,
And the white breast of the dim sea
And all disheveled wandering stars.

Yeats explained that Fergus was 'the poet of the Red Branch cycle .... He was once king of all Ireland, and, as the legend is shaped by Ferguson, gave up his throne that he might live at peace hunting in the woods. ' Notwithstanding the different versions of the legend, the fact bears out that Yeats, through this poem, tells his readers that there were kings who gave up their attachment for political power for the sake of personal peace and serenity. What ultimately triumphs through the vicissitude of life is that one should be hopeful and not fearful of one's future; that is only possible if man prizes the tender side of life more than the levers of power and influence as was the case with King Fergus.

In this context, the poem, 'Fergus and the, Druid' rendered in dialogue form ;.rings home a moral that man's destiny is composed of several dimensions, changing from one phase to another. The observation of Fergus as concluding remarks on life touches upon the irremediable destiny one has to pass through

I see my life go drifting like a river
From change to change; I have been many thinqs -
A green drop in the surge, a gleam of light
Upon a sword, a fir-tree chn a hill,
An old slave grinding at a heavy quern,
A king sitting upon a chair of gold -
And all these things were wonderful and great:
But now I have grown nothing, knowing all.
Ah : Druid, Druid, how great webs of sorrow
Lay hidden in the small slate-coloured thing i8

Fergus who was a poet as also a King of Ireland in 19 remote past in conversation with a Druid cuts a tragic ring holding that sorrow is part of one's destiny and that it just cannot be avoided.

Yeats found Irish Druidism quite seminal not only for his poetry but also for understanding Christianity in the con text of Irish lore. At a still formative age Yeats had become as familiar with the valorous Irish gods and heroes as with sligo neighbors.

'The wandering of oisin' , published in 1889, is a narrative poem using celtic heroes and great figures. In the same way, one can say that early lyrics are studded with such figures as Conchubar, Fergus , Cuchulain, Emer, Fand, the hosting Sidhe, Niamh, the Danaan children, Aengus, cumhal, and Dathi. The 1897 'Stories of Red Hanrahan' also make use of the celtic material.

As part of this research study, it may be pointed out that Yeats derived much from the writing of O'Grady Standih, Hibbert Lectures on Celtic Religion, and from Dr Douglas Hyde's work on Irish literatue, while these three authors we the main celtic influences during Yeats' subjective' feeling' period the French writer, Arbois de Jubainville may have been the main one during his more objective 'thinking and acting' period. This assessment is strengthened by Arbois' prestige, his concentration one specifically Irish rather than merely Gaulish material, and the fact that he stressed doctrines Yeats had already found congenial,

From his study of the ancient Irish lore, Yeats could make out that thee were striking parallels between the celtic religion together with Druidic belief did he reject - neither the supernatural world, nor cyclic time, nor the soul as light, nor reincarnation for a purpose, nor the possibility of initiation for those willing to pay the spiritual cost.... The point is that Druidism to him was not just a crude primitivism ; it was a higher knowledge, brought down to earth by vision, and then rationalized into a respectable system of belief not in harmonious with 'true' Christianity.

Here, it may be safely observed that he ancient Irish lore was essentially pagan in spirit. Yeats saw much merit in Christianity, not as an institutionalised religion, but in the light of his own visionary experience in which man is able to surrender his will, step by step, to the will of God. If by instinct Yeats had a love for the esoteric side of life, he found much 'luminous' material in the course of his studies in Irish lore and through personal contact.

He could not reconcile with the bourgeois pattern of living, for he wanted to experience the visible and invisible reality in all its magnificence. In this background, he found Irish mythology and folklore quite illuminating. Through his active involvement with the Irish legendary past, his mind started getting preoccupied with celtic gods such as Aengus and Edain and Mananan, son of the sea among others. It partakes of a religious emotion and it took him to the very root of Christian mysticism.

> That night I awoke lying upon my back and hearing a voice speaking above me and saying, "On human soul is like any other human soul, and therefore the love of God for any for any human soul is infinite, for no other soul can satisfy the same need in God.

It may be pointed here that Yeats wanted to sesreate the ancient glory of Ireland. His search for Irish symbols, and myths were part of his effort to make Ireland politically and culturally free. Maud Gonne records

> The land of Ireland, we (Yeats and Maud Gonne) both felt, was powerfully alive and invisibly peopled. ....If only we could make contact with the hidden forces of the land it would give us strength for the freeing of Ireland. Most of our talk centred round this and it led us both into strange places.

Yeats got leavened up his mind from time to time by the stories from Irish folklore. He has composed several poems on the basis of legends and folklore stories from Ireland. One such poem is 'The Valley of the Black Fig'.

> The dews drop slowly and dreams gathers
> unknown spears
> Suddenly hurtle before my dream-awakened eyes,
> And then the clash of fallen horsemen and the
> cries.
> of unknown perishing armies beat about my ears.
> we who still labour by the cromlech on the shore,

The grey cairn on the hill, when day sinks
drowned in dew,

Being weary of the world's empires, bow down to you,
Master of the still stars and of the flaming door.

Yeats has commented upon this poem: 'All over Ireland there are prophecies of the coming rout of the enemies of Ireland, in a certain Valley of the Black pig, and these prophecies are, no doubt, now, as they, were in the Fenian days, a political force.' when

Yeats wrote this poem, his mind was all along agog how to win the ancient glory of Ireland and this aspiration was strengthened by his study of Irish folklore. Ostensibly, Yeats celebrates, in this poem, the triumph of the Irish Armageddon over the enemies of Ireland. It is also presumed that the overtones of violence and bloodshed that make their presence felt in this poem may have something with his association with the Rosicrucian occultist MacGregor Mathers. According to a mythological interpretation of Fraser's Golden Bough and Rhys' Celtic Heathenism, a black pig may be symbolic 'of cold and winter doing battle with the summer, or of death battling with life.'

In most of his poems, apart from mystical and spiritual strains, there is a dedicated effort either to recapture the lost glory of Ireland, or to celebrate the life and emotions of common folk in such a way as to draw a symbolic meaning out of it. Illustrative of the first theme, one can refer it to three 'key' stanzas from his poem: 'The Dedication to a Book of Stories selected from the Irish Novelists.' –

There was a green branch hung with many a bell
When her own people ruled this tragic Eire;
And from its murmuring greeness,calm of Fiery,
A Druid kindness, on all hearers fell

****

Ah, exiles wandering over land and seas,
And planning, plotting always that some morrow

May set a stone upon ancestral Sorrow :
I also bear a bell-branch full of ease.
I tore it from green boughs winds tore and tossed
Until the sap of summer had grown weary :
I tore it from the barren boughs of Eire,
That country where a man can be so crossed.

And in the fifth stanza, the poet makes a revealing observation about human character (what to say of Ireland alone) by saying that when is angry and feels 'loveless', he laughs in an unrestrained but spontaneous manner; and at the same time, such a man responds movingly to the 'saddest chimes'. Feelings associated with the second theme, referred earlier, can fairly well be experienced on going through the sixth stanza of this noem. The poem as a whole echoes the spirit of Irish freedom and folklore; and it evokes some elemental emotions without any kind of ambiguity.

Similarly, the poem, 'A Dream of Death' is a representative poem with a symbolic meaning of great folklorkc interest. It is a memento to unsullied love which is prized most by common folk. The last three lines of this poem : ...'Until I carved these words: / **She was more beautiful than thy first love, / But now lies under boards**.' impart a mythic status to man's love for his woman. The beauty of the poem is that it is homely and evokes a feeling of sympathy for the man who remembers her with a feeling of pure pathos.

In the same way, one can quote with advantage some of the lines from Yeats's poem 'The Tower', specially the ones that deal with man's self-pride and self-affirmation. Yeats asseverates to own his destiny; and in itself it is a mythic gesture on his part. He is no longer tied to the ancient authority of Plato and Plotinus. He mainly relies on ' ...memories of love,/ Memories of the words of women,) .All those things whereof / man makes a superhuman / virror-resembling dream.°

It is a case of intense subjectivity; and it is in this
challenging mood, he remembers Burke and Grattan :
It is time that I wrote my will;

I choose upstanding men
That climb the streams until
The fountain leap, and at dawn
Drop their cast at the side
of dripping stone; I declare
They shall inherit my pride,
The pride of people that were
Bound neither to Cause nor to State,
Neither to slaves that were spat on,
Nor to the tyrants that spat,
The people of Burke and of Grattan
That gave, though free to refuse –
Pride, like that of the morn,
When the headlong light is loose,
or that of the fabulous horn,
or that of the sudden shower,
when all streams are dry,
or that of the hour
when the swan must fix his eye
Upon a fading gleam,
Float out upon a long
last reach of the glittering stream
And there sing his last song.

Yeats's point is that when man truly lives out the agony of one's bitter soul he is able to create his own heaven or 'Translunar Paradise', as Yeats termed it. 'The Tower' is a poem which creates 'Yeatsian' myth. His life and art get fused. Relevantly enough , the poem was written (published in 1923) during the matured phase of poet's life. "'The Tower' represented Yeats in all his moods and vacillations; it was the perfect and unique background for all aspects of his character and interests. The public aspects of his life gave him the directions he had often lacked, the sense of sharing in those public and literary heritages which he had earlier scorned. To a certain degree he became a member of a community, and paradoxically enough, attempted to graft the old virtues of his own race on to the new experiment of the Free State."

Yeats had acquired a legendary profile by virtue of his ceaseless guest to know the occult regions of life, to recover the ancient glory of Ireland and to make the composition of poetry a hieratic task. All these three elements get eloquently fused in his poem, 'The Tower'. The first four lines

What shall I do with this absurdity –
O heart, O troubled heart - - this caricature,
Decrepit age that has been tied to me
As to a dog's tail ?

Carries a note of disillusionment of one's getting old and a feeling of desolation to the extent one is at odds with the pace of emerging things. But the poet like William Blake who has influenced much, is apperceptively aware –

Never had I more
Excited, passionate, fantastical
Imagination, nor an ear and eye
That more expected the impossible –

Because he is imaginatively alive of not only of his soul's potentialities but also of his experiences that remained ingrained in his mind right from his childhood. The lines that refer to Ben Bulben and early easy days are followed by – 'It seems that I must bid the Muse go back, / Choose Plato and Plotinus for a friend / Until imagination, ear and eye, / can be content with argument and deal / In abstract things; to be derided by / A sort of battered kettle at the heel' are illustrative of Yeats's lingering mood of doubt and dreariness; but Yeats does not want to get tied down by the burden of doubt and frustration. For example, in the first stanza of the second stanza of this poem, he works out his way how to shake up his stupor :

I pace upon the battlements and stare
on the foundations of a house, or where
Tree, like a scoty finger, starts from the earth;
And send imagination forth
Under the day's declining bea, and call
Images and memories

From ruin or from ancient trees,
For I would ask a question of them all.

Yeats relies on the recuperative power of imagination, and recalls his association with his earlier surroundings and the people who made him remember, either historical real or f'ictive (about which a reference has been already drawn in the footnote No. 33, on the previous page); — for he knew that the experience of a philosopher, like plat or Plotinus would be a poor recompense to the life that is warm and full-blooded linked as it is to the circumambient universe. But, as Yeats has looked at it, he as a great artist and is conscious enough to live up to the classical virtues, such as pride, integrity and freedom to stand up to one's deepest convictions.

His interest in esoteric excursions and Irish folklore and myths was obviously owing to his personal involvement with the deeper questions of man and his destiny. Partly from his instinctive liking for occult experiences and partly on account of his intense love for Ireland, he got deep into the study of Irish myths and legendary stories, he could see life in historical continuity with mythic solemnity, as one finds in poems grouped in 'The Tower' series. Yeats goes for Irish folklore and occult practices to strengthen the bases of life on which to scaffold the architecture of his art. It is through the sensibility-buffeted and mind-scrutinised flash of wisdom, Yeats avers: 'Hunchback and saint and Fool are the last crescents' it does mean that life-wisdom is not decipherable in neat equation for 'The soul begins to tremble into stillness, To die into the labyrinth of itselfl One must live through the vital equations of life, veiled and unveil both, to know and understand the flashes of wisdom.

In the poem, 'The Saint and the Hunchback'

Yeats makes 'saint' observe :

God tries each man
According to a different plan.
I shall not cease to bless because
I lay about me with the taws

That night and morning I may thrash
Greek Alexander from my flesh,
Augustus Caesar, and after these
That great rogue Alcibiades.

The idea that is most palpable here is that one must live out the history imaginatively, live out the great men of the past – Alexander the Great (356-323 B.C.), king of Macedonia and conqueror of much of Asia: Gaius Julius Caesar Octaviamus (63 s.C.- A.D.14), first Roman emperor; and Alcibiades (ca. 450-404 B. C.), Athenian statesman and general . The validity of 'saint's' observation can only be appreciated from a high point of imagination. Essentially, poetry is a language of symbols. The poet appreciates history in symbolic terms: and then makes revealations out of the subject-matter of history and mythology. Yeats took into account this aspect when he wrote : 'A symbol is indeed the only possible expression of some invisible essence, a trans-parent lamp about a spiritual flame; while allegory is one of many possible representations of an embodied thing, or familiar principle, and belongs to fancy and not to imagination: the one is a revelation, the-46 other an amusement.' Yeats interpreted history and its makers in symbolic terms.

Yeats at one stage observed that 'whatever the great poets had affirmed in their finest moments was the nearest we could come to an authoritative religion' (Autobiography,). Here we get to the motivation of Yeats's interest in esoteric doctrines. The starting point was aesthetic: Yeats – a born poet – was conscious of the extraordinary power of works of art, an emotional and intellectual power, a power of evocation which could not be accounted for through logical and rational means. It was this very unaccountability, the way in which a work of art defies the analysis of reason, that suggested the existence in it of some secret force. vor a boy brought up in the wild legends of fairies and dhouls still current in the Irish countryside, it was natural to associate the secret power of art with that of magic.'

Yeats used Irish symbols and those of other countries in a meaningful manner and wherever he could not act access to the existing ones, he put the words and images in such a manner as to project a mythic viewpoint to what he felt and thought. There are a number of poems with Irish background in which symbols and myths from Ireland are too conspicuous to be missed. They are 'The Hosting of the Sidhe', 'The Madness of King Goll', 'The Stolen Child", most of 'The Rose' poems, those classified under 'The wind Among the Reeds', 'In the Seven woods, 'The Green Helmet and other Poems' 1910, 'Responsibilities' 1914, 'The wild Swans at coole', 1919; 'Michael Robartes and the Dancer', 1921; "The Tower' 1928

'The Winding Stair and Other Poems' 1933, 'Parnell's Funeral and Other Poems',1935; 'New Poems', 1939; 'Last Poems, 1939-1939 along with 'Narrative and Dramatic' poems; as well as those published after the death of the poet. Ireland and Irish spirit is the recurring theme in Yeats's poetic works.

But what is most striking with Yeats is his contrived deftness in etching the pulsing spontaneity of his feeling and thought fed upon the ancient lore of wisdom, philosophy and occultism without being cut of from the cross-currents of contemporary events. In this background, he needs to be merited, specially in terms of the second stanza of the poem, 'The Second Coming': 'Surely some revelation is at hand / Surely the second coming is at hand. The Second Coming ! Hardly are these words out / When a vast image out of Spiritus mundi and as one negotiates through his choice Mallarmean type images of a fabulous beast in the desert and comes to the fifth line from the end –

> but now I know
> That twenty centuries of stony sleep
> Were vexed to nightmare by a rocking cradle,
> And what rough beast, its hour come round at last,
> Slouches towards Bethlehem to be born?

There may be several interpretation to the concluding lines, but more than deciphering its literal meaning, one has to admire Yeats's creativity in taking us out of this banal age to have a new awareness about the climacteric personality of Jesus in the setting:

'Things fall apart; the centre cannot hold; / Mere anarchy is loosed upon the world, This poem abounds in choice images – each having symbolic momentum and dynamically liked to one another. In this way, the poem as a whole caries a mythic grandeur not to be out- done by the ravages of time. Thus, one can say that Yeats had a mythic and symbolic potential to create poetry of lasting value.

CHAPTER – IV

PERSONAL SYMBOLS AND MYTHS

In Yeats, apart from the abiding questions of life in terms of different mythologies, philosophy and religious interests that the poet had at different dimensions of his awareness; war, politics and love did also play a vital role; and as a result, his poetry coruscates with images and symbols. Emotionally and intellectually, he had hardly a few peers in poetic vigour and intensity in his own time – with the lone exception of Robert Frost. This was partly attributable to diverse interests he had in life and letters. The poet strove hard to fuse the wisdom of the philosophers without turning back to the saltiness of common life. writing to Dorothy Wellesley.

> This difficult work, which is being written
> everywhere now... has the substance of
> philosophy and is a delight to the poet with
> his professional pattern; but it is not
> your road or mine, & ours is the main road,
> the road of naturalness and swiftness and we
> have thirty centuries upon our side. we alone
> can 'think like a wise man, yet express ourselves
> like the common people.'

In whatever way, he was deeply influenced, he utilised that experience creatively in a symbolic manner in his writings. He had emotional bonds with Maud Gonne , Florence Farr Emery (1869-1917), English Actress; Lady Augusta Gregory (1852-1932), Yeats's close friend and collaborator devoted to the cause of Irish Nationalism; and Dorothy wellesley (1889-1956), English

Poet and friend of Yeats in the late 1930s. – are, in one way or another, responsible for the purveyance of a number of personal symbols and myths in his poetry. Of these influences, Maud Gonne' s was most powerful. His bonds with this lady of ravishing beauty who left the society of the Viceregal Court for Dublin Nationalism? 'alchemised' Yeats' s thoughts and feelings throughout his eventful literary career. Iseult Gonne, daughter to Maud Gonne, had her own share of attraction and despair for Yeats, since it was also a case of unrequited passion for the poet. However, the impact of this relationship was not as powerful as that of Maud Gonne.

Even after marriage with Joha Macbride, in 1903, Yeats remained under her spell. In most of the poems grouped under The Green Helmet (1910), the love-theme is quite perceptible. Yeats's mind appears to be dominated by the shadow of Maud Gonne in one form or another. The poet resigns to the inevitable as one gets to know from his feelings expressed in poems 'No Second Troy' and 'Reconciliation's The extract from 'No Second Troy' below is preceded his references to Mand gonne's pervasive influence on Irish political life. The reason was that she had a fascinatiag personality; and precisely for this reason he compares her to Helen of Troy :

What could have made her peaceful with a mind That nobleness made simple as a fire, kith beauty like a tightened line change bow,a kind That is not natural in with an age like this, Being high and solitary and most stern? why, what could she have done, being what she is? Was there another Troy for her to burn ?

The lines from his poem 'Reconciliation' are revealing enough to show that the poet was deeply touched on her marriage to Macbride

Some may have blamed you that you look away The verses that could move them on the day When, the ears being deafened, the sight of the eyes blind with lightning, you went from me, and I could find Nothing to make a song about but kings,

Helmets, and swords, and half-forgotten things That were like memories of you:-

But, dear, cling close to me; since you were gone, My barren thoughts have chilled me to the bone.

Here , the poet is candid enough to admit his deep-rooted emotive bonds for Maud Gonne Yeats, being responsive to the pagan approach to life in his effort to strengthen the life-bases of Christianity, all along toyed with the possibility of harmonising the claims of carnality with that of spirituality and occultism. Maud Gonne fairly well understood the psychic parameter of Yeats when he told him : 'The world should thank me for not marrying you'4 Instinctively, she was justified in saying so

because even though he felt bitter sometimes over her marital bonds with John Macbride, he turned inward and developed a rocky sense of life. His theory of masks helped him to develop newer areas of experience, as it was also so with Ezra Pound and T.S. Eliot. The remarks of Pound about the building up masks for self-expression are equally applicable to Yeats :

> In the "search for oneself", in the search
> for "sincere self-expression," one gropes ....
> for some seeming verity. One says "I am"
> this, that or the other, and with the words
> scarcely uttered one cease to be that thing.
> I began this search for the real in a book
> called Personae, casting off, as it were
> complete masks of the self in each poem. I
> continued in a long series of translations,
> which were but more elaborate masks.

why Yeats opted for the dialectic of self and anti-self through which he created masks as also deepened his sense of reality was necessitated out of the compulsive needs to discover his true identity and also to find appropriate expression in his poems. It is through the creative device of 'personae', Yeats saves himself from the banal sentimentalism even when it happens to be a love-theme. For example, the poems 'The Arrow' and 'words' , Presumably composed in terms of his bonds with Maud Gonne have a touch of pathos without being lost in frustration.

In terms of personal symbols, the poem 'Beautiful Lofty Things' 7 is of much significance; for, Yeats, besides Maud Gonne whom he has compared with Pallas Athena, evocatively considers O'Leary, John (1830-1907 – Irish Patriot), his own father John B. Yeats (1839-1922), Standish James O'Grady (1846-1929 – Irish historian and novelist), and , Augusta Gregory (Lady Gregory 1852-19 32 – Yeats's close friend and collaborator) as Olympians.

Similarly, a fruitful reference can be made to his poem, 'Adam's Curse' which was apparently inspired by the poet's conversation with Maud Gonne and her sister, Kathleen. Kathleen's remark 'that it was hard work being beautiful ' led to the composition of this poem. It begins with anote of tangible realism and then, it wrestles with the problem that it is hard to be beautiful :

We sat together at one summer's end,
That beautiful mild woman, your close friend,
And you and 7, and talked of poetry.
....And thereupon
That beautiful mild woman ....
Replied, 'To be born woman is to know –
Although they do not talk of it at school –
That we must labour to be beautiful.'

The last two stanzas reveal that Yeats under-stood the implications of 'Love' and 'being loved' and he is not far from the despairing reality to say:

we sat grown quiet at the name of love;
we sat the last embers of daylight die,
And in the trembling blue-green of the sky
A noon, worn as if it had been a shell

Washed by time's waters as they rose and fell
About the stars and broke in days and years.
I had a thought for no one's but your ears;
That you were beautiful, and that I strove
To love you in the old high way of love;
That it had all seemed happy, and yet we'd grown
As weary-hearted as that hollow moon,

The bracketing of 'weary-hearted' with 'that follow moon' heightens the poignancy of love and all that. The striking thing is that Yeats was able to put into good account his relationship with Maud Gonne and other ladies. He apparels the image of Maud Gonne in feminine grace with qualities rarely to be found in common women-folk. Through personal symbols the poetry of Yeats is greatly enriched.

One such poem is 'A Bronze qead'. It was inspired by the very impressive portrait of Maud Gonne by Lawrence Campbell. The poet is impelled to invest her with human and superhuman qualities; and recalls the fascinating spell she had since the days he had started knowing her :

But even at the starting post, all sleek and new,
I saw the wildness in her and I thought
A vision of terror that it must live through
Had shattered her soul. Propinquity had brought
Imagination to that pitch where it casts out
All that is not itself, I had grown wild
And wandered murmuring everywhere 'my child, my child'.

Or else I thought her supernatural;
As though a sterner eye looked through her eye
on this foul world in its decline and fall,
on gangling stocks grown great,great stocks run dry,
Ancestral pearls all pitched into a stly.
Beroic reverie mocked by clown and knave
And wondered what was left for massacre to save.

By working out a smashing contrast between the magnificence of feelings for Maud Gonne and the violence- riven low-Hitched modern democratic culture, Yeats passes out a message for the discerning reader to note the attendant difficulties of living a beautiful life.

Yeats was a great creative poet, conscious of the aristocracy of mind and intellect. Consequently, as he grew in age, he became conscious of the advancing old age, he developed the spirit of nonchalance and defiance in the face of adverse circumstances. In terms of this growing awareness, he found the approach of Nietche towards life interesting and rewarding, for the German philosopher held that in old age one should be interested more in enjoying the subtle quirks and shades of thinking than in testing their validity. Nietzche in The Dawn of Day observed: 'This leads them to make their thoughts palatable and enjoyable and to take away their dryness coldness and want of flavour; and thus it comes about that the old thinker apparently raises himself above his life's work, while in reality he spoits it by infusing into it a certain amount of fantasy, sweetness, flavour, poetic mists and mystic lights. This is Low Plato ended and .....

It shows that Yeats was getting, more and more unconcerned with the fateful consecLuences of life and destiny, as is made specifically clear in the last stanza of this poem :

'The work is done', grown old he thought,
'According to my boyish plan;
Let the fools rage, I swerved in nought,
Something to perf ection brought,'
But louder sang that ghost 'what then?'

The last line of this poem shows that Yeats was staking everything to build up integrity, open and defiant, like Olympians. This was because in his matured refrain of thought, as he grew old, his energy and vigour took to a reflective turn and got sharpened as a consecuence. The poem, 'An Acre of Grass' is significant for the way in which Yeats's mind reflectively worked. To quote the second stanza:

My temptation is quiet.
Here at life's end
Neither loose imagination,
Nor the mill of the mind
Consuming its rag and bone,
Can make the truth known.

To shore up his determination, he draws upon Shakespeare's literary characters : Timon and Lear who express in a highly intensive form certain facets of life which defy the very elements of reality. The remaining part of the third stanza, and the fourth one may be reproduced here to show that William Blake and Michaelengeo sustained Yeats's spirit from time to time :

or that william Blake
Who beat upon the wall
Till truth obeyed his call;

A mind Michael Angelo knew
that can pierce the clouds
or inspired by frenzy
Blake the dead in their shrouds;
Forgotten else by mankind
An old man's eagle mind.
Eul of his friendship with Dorothy wellesley,

Yeats hammers home a piece of sterling advice to the poetess to maintain her womanly dignity, the last six lines have a mythic ring, and hence, are quoted, forit also shows that Yeats had a very high regard for woman's destiny :

What climbs the stair?
Nothing that common women ponder on
If you are worth my hope ! Neither Content
Nor satisfied Conscience, but that great family
Some ancient famous authors misrepresent,
The Proud Furies each with her torch on high.

Whoever helped Yeats in realising his poetic destiny, he or she found a place of distinction in the temple of his poetry. Here it is a case of Lady Augusta Gregory who by dint of her magnanimity, foresight and courage made it possible for Yeats to pass through one of the most difficult phases of his life. Out of gratitude to Lady Gregory, he composed 'Coole Park, 1929' while the first and last stanza may be quoted in full with the last three lines from the third one to serve as a preface to the well-meaning friendship he had with Lady Gregory. when Yeats says 'They came like swallows', it means the people who got responsive patronage of Lady Gregory; it is in this context, he says that they

Found certainty upon the dreaming air,
The intellectual sweetness of those lines
That cut through time or cross it withershins.

The wording of 'Coole Park, 1929' and 'coole and Ballylee, 1931' does show that Yeats had genuine feelings of gratitude to his patron, friend and philosopher. A Woman like Lady Augusta Gregory is a product of a long process of high culture; and this was recognised by the poet in her personality. –

I mediate upon a swallow's flight,
Upon an aged woman and her house,
A sycamore and lime tree lost in night
Although that western floud is luminous,
Great works constructed there in nature's spite
For scholars and for poets after us,
Thoughts long knitted into a single thought,
A dance-like glory that those walls begot.
(I stanza)
Here, traveller, scholar, poet, take your stand
When all those rooms and passages are gone,
When nettles wave upon a shapeless mound
And samplings root among the broken stone,
And dedicate – eyes bent upon the ground,
Back turned upon the brightness of the sun
And all the sensuality of the shade
A moment's memory to that laurelled head.
(IV stanza)

From the fourth stanza, it is clear that the peculiar magic or spell of Lady Gregory that shed warmth and understanding in the environs of Coole Park. Yeats's was not a blind adulation of Maud Gonna and Lady Gregory. He remembered them with gratitude in the context of other things, for the life-panorama is not exhausted in one dimension only. There are thousand and one interlinked tissues of life which make love and friendship pleasurable and meaningful. He disagreed with the general opinion of the Rhymers' Club, formed in 1391 holding that what mattered was only energy and passion. Disagreeing with it, Yeats observed :

They (the Rhymers) had taught me that violent energy, which is like a fire of straw, consumes in a few minutes the nervous vitality, and is useless in the arts. Our fire must burn slowly, and we must constantly turn away to think, constantly analyse what we have done, be content even to have little life outside our work, to show, perhaps, to other men as little as the watch-mender shows, his magnifying glass caught in his screwed-up eye. Only then do we learn to conserve our vitality, to keep our mind enough under control and to make our technique sufficiently flexible for expression of the emotions of life as they arise.

Since Yeats was intensely involved in the contemporary issues of Irish Nationalism, he found in personal symbols and myths the most powerful source for incarnating the various shades of thoughts and feeling in his poetry. Apparently, with this idea in mind, he wrote : 'I am the first to substitute for biblical or mythological figures, historical movements men and actual and women. He was a fervent believer in full-blooded humanism and man's destiny. Precisely, he appreciated Nietzsche and the French symbolists who explored the possibility of strengthening the life-bases of Christian civilization through the living symbols and myths. Yeats found his relationship with men and women close to him fruitful not only for his existential despair but also for literary expression.

In Yeats filtered his relationship with close friends and individuals; and he could do so, because Yeats, the artist, wore masks only to avail experience in all its complexity. Yeats cosseted with ideas ranging from Occultism to the half-obscure Irish folklore without being count cut-off from the main cross-currents of modern European philosophy and literature. Given to a sceptic bent of mind, he visualised through his poetry the standpoint that one just cannot know the truth; but one can feel about it. It is in this context he found the element of suggestibility in symbols and symbolic mode of expression quite fruitful for any artist. "Yeats indeed goes so far as to maintain that 'a continuous indefinable symbolism' is 'the substance of all style' (The Symbolism of Poetry, 1980); and for him the excellence of a symbol consists in the suggestiveness that derives from the suppression of a metaphor's directly apprehensible terms of reference: 'as a sword-blade may flicker with the light of burning towers", so the symbol evokes unseen worlds."

This is a fairly objective assessment of Yeats's penchant for symbols and myths in his poetry. Since personal relationship and friendship with men and women eminent in their own ways constituted the sheet-anchor of his life, he drew creative sustenance from the life-style of his close friends. while Maud Gonne and Lady Gregory in one way or another have coloured Yeats's life and letters, there are other persons too who have touched the core of Yeats's feelings. A few selected lines from his poem, 'In Memory of Eva Gore-Booth and Con Markievicz'

carry a note of elegy and at the same, the poet through the juxtaposition of choice images intensify the suggestiveness

Pictures of the mind, recall
That table and the talk of youth,
Two girls in silk kimonos, both
Beautiful, one a gazelle.

Dear shadows, now you know it all,
All the folly of a fight
with a common wrong or right.

The innocent and the beautiful
Have no enemy but time;
Arise and bid me strike a match
And strike another till time catch;
Should the conflagration climb,
Run till all the sages know
We the great gazebo built,
They convicted us of guilt,
Bid me strike a match and blow.

The last two lines are intensely suggestive in their meaning; and the moral apparently indicates that the poet wrests the initiative from sages as he affirms his own freedom to feel and think in true human terms. A host of feelings are connated in the above few lines; and for a man of sensibility it is not difficult to decipher the purity of feelings with which the two girls, typically committed to the Irish ideals, are remembered.

In this way, one finds the validity of Lawrence's observation on myth and symbol: 'And the images of myth are symbols. They don't mean something'. They stand for unite of human feeling, human experience. A complex of emotional experience is a symbol. And the power of the symbol is to arouse the deep emotional self, and the dynamic self, beyond comprehension. Many ages of accumulated experience still throb within a symbol. And we throb in response.'

Yeats's poetry, there is a projection of distilled experience in all its emotional complexity; and he does so, by taking recourse to myths, Irish and from other countries, mainly from the Graeco-Romanic background. It is more so in Yeats's later poetry because the thoughts and feelings are expressed scintillatingly in direct and simple style. If one cares to ponder over the third stanza, specially its first five lines, the entire fourth and fifth stanzas, one would find that around the memory of Lady Gregory Augusta's son, Lady Gregory, John Synge, the poet has woven a living segment of life, contemporaneous and at the same time echoing and re-echoing meanings beyond the ordinary frontiers of time and space :

Heart smitten with emotion I sink down
My heart recovering with covered eyes;
Wherever I had looked I had looked upon
My permanent or impermanent images;
Augusta Gregory's son; . ... (III)

Mancini's portrait of Augusta Gregory
'Greatest since Rembrandt', according to
John Synge;

A great ebullient portraint certainly;
But where is the brush that could show
anything
And I am in despair that time may bring
Approved patterns of women or of men
But not that selfsame excellence again. IV
And here's John Synge himself,that rooted man
'Forgetting human words', a grave deep face
You that would judge me do not judge alone
This book or that come to this hallowed place,
Where my friends' portraits hang and look
thereon;
Ireland's history in their lineaments trace;
Think where man's glory most begins and ends
And say my glory was I had such friends. (VII)

The most striking impression one gets out of the above excerpts is that the poet succeeds in projecting the glory of Ireland through personal bonds and associations. It constitutes a veritable tour de force. In terms of personal symbols and myths, Yeats's poem under 'The Tower' are eloquent for his maturity of style and concentrated exession. Published in 1928, these poems do reveal that Yeats as he grew in age, he also grew in wisdom and understanding. Allusions to different persons are indirectly referred to ; but the main charm of these poems is that the deep cogitations of life and destiny make one pause and reflect that true poetry saves man from utter dereliction and chaos which is another name for unredeemed reality. It is true for Yeats as also for Robert Frost whose trenchant observation may also be excerpted here

The figure a poem makes .... It begins in delight, it inclines to impulse, it assumes direction with the first line laid down, it runs a course of lucky events, and ends in a clarification of life... in a momentary stay against confusion. It has denouement.

Basically, a good poem is symbolic, and to this extent, it makes us aware of the vital questions of life. In this respect, Yeats acquits superb; and the validity of which bears out in the following few lines ;

Into the labyrinth of another's being;
Does the imagination dwell the most
Upon a woman won or woman lost?
If on the lost, admit you turned aside
From a great labyrinth out of pride,
Cowardice, some silly over-subtle thought
or anything called conscience once;
And that if memory recur, the sun's
Under eclipse and the day blotted out .

These lines have a subtle shades of thought -end feeling on one's psychic response to love and woman along with attendant options one is left with. From the standpoint of symbolic importance, the poem 'All Souls' Night' is of great relevance here. Yeats is able to fuse' diverse feelings about W.T. Horton, Florence Farr, and MacGregor Mathers with remarkable felicity. The beginning is dramatic; and it sets the pace for the poet to weave a texture of remembrance about persons who influenced Yeats in one form or another. Short extracts are necessary in support of this observation :

Midnight has come and the great Christ
Church bell
And many a lesser bell sound through
the room,
And it is All Soul's Night.

And two long glasses brimmed with muscatel
Bubble upon the table. A ghost may come;
For it is a ghost's right,
His element is so fine
Being sharpened by his death,
To drink from the wine-breath
While our gross palates drink from
the whole wine.

Yeats makes us aware that occultism has its own place in life. W.T. Horton exercised a powerful influence

on Yeats in terms of poet's adventure in occultism and the mystery of life :

Horton's the first I call. He loved
strange thought
And knew that sweet extremity of pride
That's called platonic love,

And that to such a pitch of passion wrought Nothing could bring him, when his lady died, Anodyne for his love.

Words were but wasted breath;
one dear hope had he:
The inclemency Of that or the next winter would be death.

In the same way, being an ardent admirer of Florence Emery Parr, he gives an intimate 'in-view, of the efforts of this lady to fight the disintegrating forces. In this context, of the two stanzas oft Florence Farr, one may be quoted to show Yeats's high regard for this actress :

One Florence Emery I call the next,
Who finding the first wrinkles on a face
Admired and beautiful,
And by foreknowledge of the future vexed;
Diminished beauty, multiplied commonplace;
Preferred to teach a school
Away from neighbor or friend,
Among dark skins, and there

Permit foul years to wear
Hidden from eyesight to the unnoticed end.

Then, in the lines,
'I call MacGregor Mathers from his grave,
For in my first hard spring-time
we were friends,
Although of late estranged.
Inthought him half a lunatic,
half knave,
And told him so, but friendship never ends;
And what if mind seem changed,
And it seem changed with the mind,
When thoughts rise up unbid
on generous things that he did
And I grow half contented to be blind :

Yeats acknowledges that the spirit of friendship over-comes all attitudinal differences between individuals. The strains of obscurity in other stanzas imparts mythical gravity to the thoughts and feelings the poet was labouring at.

Like his personal friends, Yeats developed great liking for some great men of Irish politics. He has made admiring references to Roger Casement, O'Rahilly and Parnell, who influenced him deeply on one count or another.

In the poem 'Roger Casement', Yeats comes out as a man of action in the sense that he blames the British Government for scandalising and denigrating the image of this Irish patriot. 31 The first, second and last stanzas of this poems are worth quotable :

I say that Roger Casement
Did what he had to do,
He died upon the gallows
But that is nothing new. (I)

Afraid they might be beaten
Before the bench of Time
They turned a trick by forgery
And blackened his good name. (II)
come speak your bit in public
That some amends be made
To this most gallant gentleman
That is in quick-lime laid. (last)

Yeats is very much exercised mentally over the foul manner Roger Casement was perjured; and precisely, in the fifth stanza, the poet calls public to 'desert the perjurer' s side' Another of

Yeats's poem, 'The Ghost of Roger Casement' is significant; for, in making a use of personal symbol, the poet has been able to hammer home a historical judgement on British imperialism and the cussed attitude of its administrators towards the subjugated people:

John Bull has gone to India
And all must pay him heed
For histories are there to prove
That none of another breed
Has had a like inheritance,
....
The ghost of Roger Casement
Is beating on the door

In the five lines from the third stanza, followed by the two-line refrain (after every stanza, Yeats is able to link the untimely foul death of Roger 35 Casement with the arrogance of John Bull. The fourth stanza is still more dramatic because Yeats has been able to adapt Gray's Elegy to his viewpoint :

I poked about a village church
And found his family tomb
And copied out what I could read
In that religious gloom;
But fame and virtue pot.
Draw round and raise a shout;

The ghost of Roger Casement
Is beating on the door

The repetition of the two-line refrain, after every stanza, heightens the dramatic value of this poem: and at the same time, Yeats wants to point out that the foul deeds must get back retribution at appropriate time.

Similarly, the elegiac paean sung on the death of 'o' 'Rahilly', one of the rebels shot during the Easter Rebellion in 1916 immortalises his name. The reiteration of the homely question 'How goes the weather?', after every stanza, heightens the bitter feelings Yeats entertained on the sad events. The last stanza has a tragic note s 'What remains to sing about / But of the death he met / Stretched under a doorway / Somewhere off Henry Street; / They that found him found upon / The door above his head / 'Here died the O'Rahilly/ R.I.P.' writ in blood." — followed by the refrain : 'How goes the weather ?

Before ending this chapter, it would be -relevant to refer to the poems : 'Parnell's Funeral' and 'Come Gather Round Me Parnellites' from the viewpoint of personal symbols and myths. Yeats is able to make a good use of his personal relationships, direct or otherwise, with different individuals because he scrupulously cares to decipher their contribution to some of the basic human values in which Yeats was ardently interested throughout his life.

CHAPTER - V

YEATS'S APPROACH TO NATURE AND HISTORY

Yeats was first and foremost a great poet; and he maintained his power of creativity upto the end of his life. From his early infancy, if Yeats was a visionary he was also full of ebullience for enjoying life and for understanding it in all its amplitude. Being a man of refined instincts and passionate fury, he had no taste for any kind of colour-less interpretation of history. In the same way, his response to nature was not that of wordsworth but was that of a man who considered nature a part of the cosmic process across the ages. Nature provided man with symbols and images to live a meaningful life even in the midst of inhospitable and hostile forces. This is how Yeats felt as it is borne out in his poems. Just to cite an example, even a not well-known poem, 'A woman's beauty is like a white' shors that Yeats revealed the memorable facets of humanity by drawing upon symbols from nature and history. In this way his message gets eloquent :

A woman's beauty is like a white
Frail-bird, like a white sea-bird alone
At daybreak after stormy night
Between two furrows upon the ploughed lands
A sudden storm, and it was thrown
Between dark furrows upon the ploughed land.
How many centuries spent

The sedentary soul
In toils of measurement
Beyond eagle or mote,
Beyond hearing or seeing,
or Archimedes' guess,
To raise into being
That loveliness ?

The second stanza of this poem is all the more meaningful and weighty in the sense that the poet, through the sheer power of imagination, silhouettes the corning into being a sea-shell in the morning; and then its being destroyed overnight by the storm; then he draws an inference framed in interrogation the different factors that go to bring about 'loveliness' be it of a woman or that of a sea-shell. Nature serves as foil, for the poet to project a world-view much more richer and broader in scope than that of the conventional notion of history.

It may be pointed out here that Yeats's approach towards nature and history was coloured by the mythopoeic vision of civilisation. Since history, to Yeats, is not the more chronicling of important events, he drew upon diverse sources of religion and philosophy in the framing of ' A Vision'. 2 Leaving aside the personal factors like the death of John MacBride, husband to Maud Gonne whom he loved intensely; her illness and being disturbed as well as the failure of Yeats's overtures to Iseult Gonne (daughter to Maud Gonne) for marriage, Yeats after his marriage with Georgie Hyde-Lees on 20th October 1917 found a way out of his emotive distractions when he came to know that his wife practised 'automatic writing' revealed to her by the communicators from the spirit world.

In point of reality, 'A Vision' is a fulfilment of Yeats's desire to have a philosophical system to aid him in his poetry. 'I wished for a system of thought that would leave my imagination free to create as it chose and yet make all that it created, or could create, part of the one history, and that the soul's.'

The fragmentary revelations by the spirits which make the reading of 'A. Vision' sufficiently interesting though at times obscure provided Yeats 'metaphore for poetry'.

Apparently, Yeats's effort to discover a philosophical system of his own in 'A Vision' catalysed his imagination greatly, the effect of which one finds in such powerful poems as 'The Second Corning' (1919) and 'The Tower' (1929). This philosophical venture triggered Yeats's imagination to visualise his poem, 'Leda and the Swan' which convey poet's disenchantment with the contemporary civilisation

> 'After the individualist, demagogic movement, founded by Hobbes and popularised by the Encyclopaedists and the French Revolution, we have a soil so exhausted that it cannot grow crop again for centuries.' Then I thought, 'Nothing is now possible but some movement from above preceded by some violent annunciation.' My fancy began to play with Leda and the Swan for metaphor.... '

The sonnet 'Leda and the swan', on its publication, shook up the deadened sensibility of some of the conservative readers. This poem describes grippingly the plight of woman caught in the act of brutalised love. 'The distress of Leda is emphasised by the double question which takes up the whole of the second quatrain,7 where the verb 'push' and the noun 'rush' stress the intense brutality of the rape in contrast with the weakness and terror of 'those terrified vague fingers'. Note how physically precise is that Angle* Saxen noun 'shudder' contrasted with the latinate and abstract verb 'engenders! : Leda is reduced from 'girl' to mere 'body', the physical means by which terror enters history.'

By interpreting the mythological story of 'Leda and the Swan' in the context of the happenings in the twentieth century world, Yeats shook not only the complacency of his readers but also made them think deeply upon the basic issues involved in male and female relationship. The point is that even a single act of brutality may trigger actions, reactions and their consequences beyond the immediate periphery of a particular happening.

Through this myth-impregnated sonnet, Yeats expresses his deeply cherished feelings about the implications of lone through violence. Even a single act of violence has its far-reaching repercussions on the course of civilisation. For men of mob-thinking, ordinary acts of violence are just the order of the day. They take human life just a scrappy thing. For theft, there is no myth, nor any history. They live through the moment; and ignore the fact that even a split-second momentary act, if it is unthought and reflected, has a shadow lingering across centuries. This is what is implied by Yeats :

> I imagine the annunciation that founded
> Greece as made to Leda, remembering that
> they showed in a Spartan temple, strung up
> to the roof as a holy relic, on unhatched egg
> of hers; and that from one of her eggs came
> Love and from the other War. But all things are
> from antithesis, and when in my ignorance I
> try to imagine what older civilisation that
> annunciation rejected I can but see bird and
> woman blotting out some corner of the Babylonian
> mathematical insight.

It is a way of looking at history from a much deeper perspective going beyond mere utilitarian approach. By a sheer stroke of insight, Yeats interprets the course of ancient civilisation through the mazes of Leda and the Swan myth. It does also illustrate the Yeatsian view that the human civilisation works out its destiny through the inter-reaction of opposite elements. Yeats has a cyclic notion of history governed by the inter-acting and reacting opposite forces – mainly arising out of the interplay of primary phases linked to antithetical phases in various ways on men and women governed by the Four Faculties and Four Principles. (The principal symbol employed Yeats is 'The Great wheel' with twenty-eight incarnations disgrammatically shown on its circumference. On it are marked four circles – the top one for 'East' representing 'Breaking of Strength', the bottom for 'west' carrying the notion of 'discovery of strength' ; and the 'South' is represented by a circle on the right, while the circle on the left connote the 'North'. Perpendicularly, the wheel is divided into two sections – one on the left indicates 'Primary phases': and the one on the right is of 'Antithetical phases'. For this reason, the four circles on the circumference of the wheel are affected by these two types of phases, the circle of 'East' at the top; and that of 'West' at the bottom are shaded in left half; and the right half remains blank, implying a sense of 'white'. As against this, the circle on the left side is of North and it is ahaded completely; and it means 'Complete Objectivity'; whereas the circle on the right side of the Great Wheel is of 'South' and it signifies the characteristics of 'Complete Objectivity'.

The chief characteristics of 'Primary phases' is 'passivity'; and that of 'Antithetical Phases' is 'Unity of Being'. The two transversal lines passing through the center of 'The Great wheel' and cutting through the circumference at four points has indicatorss 'Head' and 'Loin' – the former on the side of Anti-thetical Phases' while the latter on the 'Primary Phases'. These transversal lines cutting through the downward segment of the circumference are named 'Fall', through the 'Primary Phases' and 'Heart', through the ' Anti-thetical Phases'.

If one reflects over the chief indicators of 'The Great Wheel' and visualises the inter-acting work-ing of the Four Faculties and the Four Principles one would find that the physical and metaphysical stuff of life is a result of this inter-action and reaction on a personal and cosmic level. The ascent of the soul and its descent in this mortal body depends upon a host of discords, oppositions and contrasts as also on their reconciliation. It does not take place in ascertainable neat numerical equations but through a very complicated process. 'Every phase is in itself a wheel; the individual soul is awakened by a violent oscillation (one thinks of Verlaine oscillating between the church and the brothel) until it sinks in on that whole where the contraries are united, the antinomies revolved.'

With this extract, as also with some others, Yeats is able to convey through 'A Vision' his view of human civilisation and the role of eminent personalities in it. As Yeats delves deeper to monitor the contours of nature and history, he finds from his own tense struggles arising out of his failure on love account vis-a-vis Maud Gonne as well as with her adopted daughter, Iseult Gonne, violent setbacks to Irish independence that the struggle within a person is in terms of the self versus anti-self. That Yeats was able to live up to this aspe6t of personal life finds expression in his poem 'Ego Dominus Tuus' in which there is a dialogue between Hic-Tics and 'Ille' defending the objective side of life while ' Ille ' endorses the claim of 'subjectivity'. The lines : I call to the Mysterious who yet / Shall walk with the wet sands to the edge of the stream / And look most like me, being indeed by double, / And prove of all imaginable things / The most unlike, being my anti- self.'

Yeats all along strove hard to come to grips with the reality. In fact the entire dialectic of self qua anti-self, or for that matter the claims of subjectivity and the compulsions of objectivity made Yeats to explore the bases of reality. Even allowing minus points of 'A Vision' in terms of sinery obscurity at places, one has to accept this philosophical essay to arrive at a deeper vision of reality. He accorded a very high place for poet who has a direct apprehension of reality and who is not satisfied with half-palliatives :

Nor has any poet I have read of or heard or met with been a The other self, the anti-self or the antithetical self, as one may choose to name it, comes but to those who are no longer deceived, whose passion is reality. The sentimentalists are practical men who believe in money, in position, in a marriage bell, and whose understandigg of happiness is to be so busy whether at work or play, that all is forgotten but the momentary aim. They find their pleasure in a cup that is filled from Lethe's wharf, and for the awakening for the vision, for the revelation of reality, tradition offers us a different word —ecstasy.'

Yeats availed the medium of prose to develop his metaphysic of life; and quite frequently, it also got expressed in his verse. In 'Ego Dominus Tuus', the differentiation in the life-outlook of a man of the world and that of an artist is succintly put forth:

For those that love the world serve
it in action,
Grow rich, popular and full of influence,
And should they paint or write, still
it is action:
The struggle of the fly is marmalade,
The rhetorician would deceive his neighbours,
The sentimentalist himself; while art
Is but a vision of reality.

Though the actual work on his interesting but complicated essay, 'A Vision' was started after his marriage, yet Yeats in his thinking was groping towards a religious system as he informed his father that it was more or less logically worked out. A, system, which will, I hope, interest you as a form of poetry. I find the settiing of it all in order has' helped my verse, has given me a new framework and new patterns. One goes on year after year getting the disorder of one's mind in order, and this is the real impulse to create.

A number of major poets in the twentieth century have looked with consternation the chaos that insidiously dogs their well-meaning efforts to arrive at harmony and belief. Apart from Yeats, Robert Frost and T.S. Eliot have dealt with this existential dilemma in their writings. The writing of poetry helped him to develop a world out-look full of chastened wisdom, sufficiently supple and viable to withstand the frenzied mob-feeling, as is implied by his observation s 'After the individualist, demagogic movement, founded Hobbes and popularised by the Encyclopaedists and the French Revolution, we have a soil so exhausted that it cannot grow that crop again for centuries'. Then I thought, 'Nothing is now possible but some movement from above preceded by some violent annunciation.'

These feelings find expression in his poem, 'The Second Coming'. Triggered by the violent happenings following the easter 1916 rising of the Irish nationalists against the British Government, he under-went a traumatic experience; and precisely, his poetic sensibility could conceive only something like specalypse. The poet is fearful of the turn of sad events. With intense agony, Yeats felt that the term of events was not conducive to the civilised and cultured mode of living, as it has been expressed in the first stanza of 'The Second Coming' ;

Turning and turning in the widening gyre
The Falcon cannot hear the falconer;
Things fall apart; the centre cannot held;
Mere anarchy is loosed upon the world,
The blood-dimmed tide is loosed, and everywhere
The ceremony of innocence is drowned;
The best lack all conviction,while the worst
Are full of passionate intensity.

The very few belonging to the aristocracy of thought and feeling are overwhelmed and voted out by the blood-dimmed, unregenerate masses. The second stanza: 'Surely some revelation is at hand ..../

Slouches towards Bethlehem to the born?' puts in /Slouches perspective in in a highly figurative language having mythic overtones, Yeats's apprehensions that instead of Jesus, somebody incarnating the spirit of 'Anti-Christ' would hover over the world in time to come.

whether or not his prophetic vision turned out to be literally true, the fact remains that Yeats in his own way sensed the shadow of totalitarianism, despotism and terrorism, coupled with the resurgency in dehumanising forces, as it has been patently true in Europe, between the two world Was, and the global process of dehumanisation owing to a large-scale impact of technology with its attendant pitfalls of environmental pollution, colonisation and the post-decolonisation policies of the industrially advanced countries.

As already pointed out, Yeats the poet, interpreted the contemporary history in a mood of tragic wisdom, for he was deeply involved in the cause of Irish independence; and so he could not commisorate iniquities perpetrated in the Irish people. Yeats's excursion towards the framing of 'A Vision', about which his mind was already getting ripe through his interest in Occultism, Theosophy, Mysticism, Mythology, Religion beside his involvement in the masterpieces of world literature, was to a very great extent actuated by his desire to resolve the contradictions of his own despair at the turn of personal and political events and also to serve him as a viable 'intellectual reservoir' for his poetry. A knowledge. able commentator has rightly put it :

> In 1917, Yeats married Georgiana Hyde-Lees.
> Between 1917 and 1920 her automatic writing
> and speech gave Yeats the raw material for
> 'A Vision' (1925; rev. ed., 1937), the work
> that crowned the pursuit of mystical knowledge:
> its 'stylistic arrangements of experience'
> provide a systematic geometry of human life –
> part history, part philosophy, part mysticism,
> part psychology; but wholly Yeats.

This is entirely true about 'A Vision', and this is what Yeats has tried to convey in the XVI section, of his chapter: 'The Great Year of the Ancients' :

My instructors certainly expect neither a "primitive state" nor a return to barbarism as primitivism and barbarism are ordinarily understood, antithetical revelation is an intellectual influx neither from beyond man-kind nor born of a virgin, but begotten from our spirit and history.

The emphasis is on man's effort to maintain clarity in the midst of chaos and confusion that is what is available in the objective world of history. Yeats the poet yearns for a better cultural dispensation; and that is why, he thought and felt in 'trans-historical' terms. The excerpt, being reproduced (minus the technical terminology) here would show that as Yeats evaluated the cultural history of mankind in 'A Vision', from different angles of life, he found ideas and feelings which made some of his poems, like 'The second Coming' typical of the ferment in the twentieth century; and also typical of the man who reacted to the modern conditions of life as an artist who peeped through the ages and looked into the future with the quet dignity of a thoughtful and courageous aristocrat :

At the birth of Christ took place, and at the coming antithetical influx will take place, a change equivalent to the interchange of the tinctures. * Before the birth of Christ religion and vitality were polytheistic, anti-thetical, and to this the philosophers opposed their primary secular thought. Plato thinks all things into unity and is the 'First Christian'. At the birth of Christ religious life becomes

Primarys , secular life antithetical –
man gives to Caeser the things that are Caesar's.

In this extract, Yeats puts in perspective the antithetical characteristic of religious life and secular affairs. If one cares to keep in mind the subtle difference between the life-outlook of Jesus and that of Caesar and protagonists of secular power, one can appreciate Yeats's remarks in this respect s 'A primary dispensation looking beyond itself towards a transcendent power is dogmatic, levelling, unifying, feminine, humane, peace its means and end; and anti-thetical dispensation obeys imminent power, is expressive, hierarchical, multiple, masculine, harsh, surgical. 'It is with this distinction in mind, Yeats goes on to hold that 'the intellectual preparation' already begun will reach its climax at the time 'the Great Year' completes its cycle. Here, one needn't talk over the length of the Great Year; but one should try to understand Yeatsian feelings about the necessity of an inevitable change. 'Something of what I have said it must been the myth declares, for it must reverse our era and resume past eras in itself; what else it must be no man can say, for always at the critical moment the Thirteenth Cone, the sphere, the unique intervenes:

.... somewhere in sands of the desert
A shape with lion body and the head of a man,
A gaze blank and pitiless as the sun,
Is moving its slow thighs, while all about it
Reel shadows of the indignant desert birds.

That these lines are from 'The second coming': and it goes to confirm the contention of Yeats that his well-meaning attempts to systematise his own thinking would help him to chisel his thoughts and feelings for the sake of enriching his poetry. Thoughts delineated in 'A Vision' find their reiteration sometimes with better projection in his poems. The diagrammatic projection of the Great Wheel about the categorisation of human personality in terms of tweity-eight incarnations or phases of the moon through which history unrolls itself has been succintly expressed in his poem, 'The Phases of the Moon': It is rendered through the fictionalised character, Michael Robertaes who in his talk to his friend, Owen Aherne explains its

> Twenty-and-eight the phases of the moon
> The full and the moon's dark and all the crescents,
> Twenty-and-eight, and yet but six-and-twenty
> The cradles that a man must needs be rocked in;
> For there's no human life at the full or the dark.
> From the first crescent to the half, the dream
> But somrrons to adventure, and the man
> Is always happy like a bird or a beast;
> But while the moon is rounding towards the full
> He follows whatever whim's most difficult
> Among whims not impossible, and though scarred,
> His body moulded from whin his body
> Grows comelier. Eleven pass, and then
> Athena takes Achilles by the hair,
> Hector is in the dust, Nietzsche is born,
> Because the hero's crescent is the twelfth.
> And yet, twice born, twice buried, grow he must,
> Before the full moon, helpless as a worm. 30

The reference to Athena, the Olympian goddess of wisdom, and Achilles, the great Greek hero in the Trojan War as well as to Hector, the warrior on the Trojan side imply the tragic phase of history because the heroism because personalities, under the domination of heroism must come into clash with their opponents and meet their tragic end. The German philosopher, Friederich Nietzsche who was an iconoclast and hero in his own inimitable way partook of the Hellenic tragic spirit; and that is why, he has been included in the twelfth phase. The phase thirteen consummates the existential conflict within oneself, for the personality under this phase fails to get proper response in the objective world.

The thirteenth moon but sets the soul at war In its own being, and when that war's begun There is no muscle in the arm; and after, Under the frenzy of the fourteenth moon, The soul begins to tremble into stillness, To die into the labyrinth of itself:

Yeats cites the example of Baudlaire, Beardsley, Ernest Dawson belonging to 'Phase Thirteen', which ' is a phase of great importance, because the mast intellectually subjective phase, because only here can be achieved in perfection that in the antithetical which corresponds to sanctity in the primarz ; not self-denial but egression for expression's sake. Its influence indeed upon certain writers has caused them in their literary criticism to exalt intellectual sincerity to the place in literature which is held by sanctivity in theology. At this phase the self discovers, within itself, while struggling with the Body of Fate, forms of emotional morbidity which others recognise as their own; as the Saint may take upon himself the physical diseases of others. There is almost always a preoccupation with those metaphors and symbols and mythological images through which we define whatever seems most strange or most morbid. Self-hatred now reaches its height, and through this hatred comes the slow liberation of intellectual love. There are moments of triumph and moments of defeat, each in its extreme form, for the subjective intellect knows nothing of moderation.

Here, Yeats deploys a commendable insight into the processes of creativity in artists like Charles Baudlaire. Similarly, the comment on the character of Helen of Troy in his observation regarding 'Phase Fourteen', the examples of which are Keats,

Giorgione and many beantiful women of whom Helen is the most representative :

> Here are born those women who are most touching in their beauty. Helen was of the phase; and she comes before the mind's eye elaborating a delicate personal discipline as though she would make her whole life an image of a unified antithetical energy. While seeming an image of softness and of quiet, she draws perpetually upon glass with a diamond. Yet she will not number among her sins anything that does not break that personal discipline, no matter what it may seem according to others' discipline; but if she fail in her own discipline she will not deceive herself, and for all the languor of her movements, and her indifference to the acts of others, her mind is never at peace. She will wander much alone as though she consciously meditated her masterpiece that shall be at the full moon, yet unseen by human eyes, and when she returns to her house she will look upon her household with timid eyes, as though she knew that all powers of self-protection had been taken away, that of her once violent primary. tincture nothing remained but a strange irresponsible innocence. Her early life has perhaps been perilous because of that nobility The greater the peril the nearer has she approached to the final union of primary and antithetical, where she will desire nothing; already perhaps, through weekness of desire, she understands nothing yet seems to understand everything; already serves nothing, while alone seeming of service. Is it not because she desires so little, gives so little that man will die and murder in her service?

Here, Yeats with consummate skill delineates the internal processes of the legendary character of Helen and her impact on the course of events in the remote past. It may be here observed that Yeatsian approach to history is quite different to that of Karl Marx. Yeats is mainly concerned with only the aristocratic few who have changed the course of history. Yeats's approach is essentially mythopoeic, for the pull of occult also mattered with him. He did not stop thinking merely at the chronicling of historical facts alone. He could not lose sight of the occult factors. in the poem, 'The Phases of the moon' , to the query of. Aherns :

> And what of those / That last servile crescent has set free?'
> Robartes replies that in the final stage, apparently
> after the cosmic cataclysm is over
> when all the dough has been so kneaded up
> That it can take what form cook Nature fancies,
> The first thin crescent is wheeled round
> once more.

Yeats believed that after every cataclysm, nature re-begins its cycle. This implies the idea of the transmigration of soul; and the re-cycling of the world after every Great Yeat. 'In his letters to Dorothy Wellesley, Yeats talks of the spirits of the dead in folklore who are represented as being enveloped in a whirlwind. The whirling metaphor is expanded in 'The Gyres' to embrace the cyclic movement of history which includes not only the spirits of the dead, but dead cultures and civilizations as well. And, if we must further unravel the complex web of associations which the symbol of gyre carried for Yeats, there are many useful passages in A Vision. Thus, for example, in the introduction to that alleged mystical book of the sixteenth century, Yeats wrote s 'The anguish of birth and death cry out in the same instant. Life is no series of emanations from divine reason such as the Cabalists imagine, but an irrational bitterness, no orderly descent from level to level, no waterfall but a whirlpool, a gyre.'

Linked with the cyclic movement of history and the gyratory mode of progression and retrogression individually and socially both, Yeats was also led to believe in the efficacy of a mathematical form, consisting of ' a double cone', the narrow end of each cone being in the centre of the broad end of the other. It had its origin from a straight line which represents, new time, new emotion, new subjective life, and a plane at right angles to this line which represents, new space, new intellect, new objective life; while it is marked out by two gyres which represent the conflict, as it were, of plane and line, by two movements, which circle about a centre because a movement outward on the plane is checked by and in turn checks a movement (onward upon the line; and the circling is always narrowing or spreading, because one movement or other is always the stronger. in other words, the human soul is always moving outward into the objective world or inward into itself; and the movement is double because the human soul would not be conscious were it not suspended between contraries, the greater the contrast the more intense the consciousness. The man, in whom the movement inward is stronger than the movement outwards, the man who sees all reflected within himself, the subjective man, reaches the narrow end of a gyre at death, for death is always, they counted, even when it seems the result of accident, preceded by an intensification of the subjective life, The objective man on the other hand, whose gyre moves outward, receives at this moment the revelation, not of himself seen from within, for that is impossible to objective man, but of himself as if he were somebody else. This figure is true also of history, for the end of an age, which always receives the revelation of the character of the next age, is represented by the coming of one gyre to its place of greatest expansion and of the other to that of its greatest contraction. At the present moment the life gyre is so sweeping outward', unlike that before the birth of Christ which was narrowing, and has almost reached its greatest expansion. The revelation which approaches will however take its character from the contrary movement of the interior gyre. All our scientific, democratic, fact-accumulating, haterogenous civilisation belongs to the outward gyre....'

Full of penetrating insight, this extract shows that Yeats's approach to history differs greatly from that of ordinary approach, for he also takes into account the occult view of life. 'The historian thinks of Greece as an advance on Persia, of Rome as in something or other so adverse of Greece, and thinks it impossible that any man could prefer the hunter's age to the agricultural. I, upon the other hand, must think all civilisations equal at their best, every phase returns, therefore in some sense every civilisation. I think of the hunter's age and that which followed immediately at time when man/is working consciousness had not reached its resent complexity and stability. There was little fear of death, sometimes men lay down and died at will, the world of the gods could be explored easily whether through some orgiastic ceremony or in the trance of the ascetic. Apparitions came and went, bringing comfort in the midst of tragedy.'

In an another observation, Yeats makes it clear: 'Vice said that we know history because we create it, but as nature was created by God only God can know it.' It is Yeats, the visionary's remark; and one has to appreciate it at that. Evan as Yeats discussed the progress of man through the struggle between contraries and its resolution at different dimension, he equally prized the value of 'self-control' in human history. 'A civilisation is a struggle to keep self-control, and in this it is like some great tragic person, some Niobe who must display an almost superhuman will or the cry will not touch our sympathy. The loss of control over thought comes towards the end, first a sinking in upon the moral being, then the last surrender, the irrational cry, revelation — the scream of June's Peacock.' Here, the peacock's scream symbolises the end of a civilisation. It is now sufficient to say that Yeats had a much deeper view of history and nature than that of an ordinary historian. His awareness of the occult and metaphysical vision had a great bearing upon his view of man and civilisation.

CHAPTER - VI

THE SUMMING UP – THE GREATNESS OF W.B. YEATS AS A POET

In making an assessment of the topic: 'The Mythological Elements and Symbols in the writings of W.B. Yeats, it may be recalled, with reference to his own excerpts in the second chapter and elsewhere, that Yeats considered myths and symbols very important for true poetry. He held to the belief that poetry should take into account poet's aspirations, as also the creative response to his personal setbacks in terms of his multi-dimensional personality. in this respect, T.S. "Eliot, another great poet of the twentieth century English literature, also shares the same views as W.B. Yeats. Both these great poets took to poetry with religious seriousness. It is this approach that makes Yeats a great poet. His poetry coruscates with images and symbols dating from ancient period to his own era; for the poet strove hard to develop belief without for-saking the sense of beautiful.

I believe that the renewal of belief which is the great movement of our time, will more and more liberate the arts from 'their age' and from life, and leave then more and more free to lose themselves in beauty, and to busy themselves like all the great poetry of the past and like religions of all times, with 'old faiths, myths and dreams', the accumulated beauty of the age. I believe that all men will more and more reject the opinion that 'poetry is a criticism of life' and be convinced that it is a revelation of a hidden life, and be more and more convinced that it is a revelation of a hidden life, and that they may even come to think painting, poetry, and music the only means of conversing with eternity loft to man on earth.

Here, as we refer to another observation of Yeats, we find that the poet took to poetry with all the single-minded passion, for he considered it as the only way to exist as a man of delicate sensibility. 'We must ascend out of common on interests, the thoughts of the newspapers, of the market place, of men of science, but only so far as we can carry the normal, passionate, reasoning self, the personality as a whole. 'In his quest for deepening the life-processes, he availed time and energy to study ancient myths and folklore traditions of Ireland which helped him to compose poems of abiding interest. Being receptive to the visionary view of life, Yeats in his thinking transcended the petit bourgeois value-system. For him ,man was more than a bundle of bodily sensations determined by objective circumstances. Speaking of men and women of earlier ages in distant past, Yeats pointed out : 'There was little fear of death, sometimes men lay down and died at will, the world of the gods could be explored easily whether through some orgiastic ceremony or in the trance of the ascetic. Apparitions came and went, bringing comfort in the midst of tragedy.'

He maintained a fervent belief in man's destiny; and it is in terms of this thinking, he expressed ideas and feelings of men and women who dared to step out of the conventional mould while facing the perils attending to the defiance of social circumstances. It is this interest in evaluating man's encounter with his circum-stances, whether for good or bad, that made Yeats go deeper into the texture of reality. It is for this reason Yeats realised the importance of symbols and myths, which have the power of suggestiveness whereby a reader's mind gets evoked to a host of ideas and feelings quite remote to the pedestrian world of city life. Yeats's poetry has this remarkable quality in it. It has tremendous power of evoking images and feelings in readers, of which they just cannot conceive out of their native efforts. There are a number of poems which testify to the validity of this observation. Mere, a passing reference may be made to some of the poems : 'Under Saturn', 'Easter, 1916', 'The Second Coming', 'A Payer for my Daughter' under 'Michael Robartes and the Dancer' series; and from 'The Tower' series, one can cite Poems 'Sailing to Byzantium', 'The Tower' , 'Ancestral Houses', 'My Descendants', 'Nineteen Hundred and Nineteen', 'Leda and Swan', 'Among School Children', 'From Oedipus at Colonus'" and all Souls' Night', Similarly, there are other poems from other poetic titles which are evocative and scatter out images and fantasies, quite remote to the ones, one is ordinarily used to in the pedestrian run of things.

The intent and the passion with which he tried to understand the Irish folklore symbols and myths as also those of others are indicative of the higher aims he had set for his poetry. The symbolic expression :' a sword-blade may flicker with light of burning towers' attunes the mind of reader to unexpected ideas and feelings because of its suggestiveness. Myths also appealed to the poet for their symbolic worth. He was also drawn to different myths, his own country's and that of other nations out of his temperamental penchant for intuitive understanding in preference to dry abstraction and ratiocinating approach, for myth, in its primary form – regardless of its belittlement by modern mind fed on ersatz culture – is the closest verbal approach to an immediate intuition of reality.

It is true that Yeats derived much insight out of his study of the Irish Folklore. However, he introduced dramatic intensity in his way of looking at things around him and within himself through the cultivation of mask or persona in terms of different layers of his own subjectivity vis-a-vis the inter-relationship with the world oe men and things. It is essentially a dramatic device. Robert Browning used it in his 'dramatic monologue 'poems', like 'The last Ride Together', 'Rabbi Ben Ezra', and 'My last Duchess' among others; but Yeats's wearing of the 'mask' is much more subtle, dynamic and deeper than that of Browning. Yeats used the device of 'mask' to introduce density to the communication he intended to convey. For example, there is a poem 'The Mask' in 'the Green Helmet and other Poems' which is revealatory of the intent of the poet for introducing the elements of mask' or 'persona' in his poems and dramas :

'Put off that mask of burning gold
with emerald eyes.'
'o no, my dear, you make so bold
To find if hearts be wild and wise,
and yet not cold.'

'I would but find what's there to find,
Love or deceit.'
'It was the mask engaged your mind,
And after set your heart to beat,
Not what's behind.'

'But lest you are my enemy,
I must enquire.'
'o no, my dear, let all that be;
what matter, so there is but fire
In you, in me ? '

This 3-stanza poem underscores the importance of 'mask' for a sensitive individual placed in a complicated social situation of modern world. Before putting trust in a fellow-being, one's mind gets crisscrossed by various shades of doubts. This is how the poet concretizes human experience. Apparently, Yeats's psychological interest in the worth of 'mask' was sharpened as a sequel to Maud Gonne's marriage to John MacBride. Mentally it was a great setback to the poet who had believed Maud Gonne's word that she was not going to marry anyone. Thus, the need for wearing a 'mask' arose out of armouring himself against the weird uncertainties that shadowed his life from one stage to another. The poet needed it in terms of self-objectivities. Through the wearing of masks at different phases of his life and career, Yeats was fulfilling his religious and artistic needs in the sense of 'The Stages on the Way' visualized by the Danish Philosopher, Soren Kierkegaard.

The concept of 'masks' helped him to scale the ascent of his poetic pilgrimage. Since one's mind has to wander through a subjective field of weird uncertainties and fluctuating moods, the application of 'masks', with full awareness like Lord Byron in facing the tense challenges life, imparts grit and clarity to one's character.

It is in this way, Yeats introduced dramatic tension to his poems; and specially on those incidents which touched him deeply.

The close of the nineteenth century and the years that entered the twentieth century constituted a period of turmoil. Besides the uneven and uncertain pace of events concerning the Irish independence, Yeats was greatly chagrined to find that the lady on whom he had built a near-absolute trust had given a slip to him by marrying another man.Yeats was obviously puzzled; and then it dawned upon him not to trust so readily, for to negotiate with the worldly-minded people, most of them given to one form of falsity or the other, the policy of simplicity and direct belief is to expose oneself to dire consequences. Yeats had an adventurous approach towards life and that put his nerves to tune thoughts and feelings, partly tragic and partly mocking in an uncertain world. In his play, The Green helmet (1910), he touches upon this aspect :

I choose the laughing lip
That shall not turn from laughing
whatever rise or fall
The heart that grows no bitterer although
betrayed by all
The hand that loves to scatter; the life
like a gambler's throw..1

Yeats had a high sense of personality; and he cultivated it assiduously. He wanted to have autonomy for himself without being cut off from his fellow-men. It is in terms of this high aim, he developed the concept of mask as well as the notion of 'self' and 'anti-self'. In the early draft of his play, 'The Player Queen',

Yeats puts in perspective the problem of love and the uncertainties centering around it through his two characters : Yellow Martin (who adores his lady and love for her), and the other one, Peter cautions his friend in regard to his love-euphoria :

Yellow Martin : But I wish her to be all the perfection I can imagine, and would be no less myself.

Peter : Seem a little, play a little. If you are jealous try to seem trustful and happy. If you are full of gloom because she was cross with you seem lighter than a swallow. If you think her foolish, pretend that she is wisdom itself.

Yeats adopted this approach, partly from practical standpoint, and partly for chiselling his own sensibility; for, the poet tried to moniter different states of awareness: from dream to reality and 'vice versa. In this endeavour, his tuning of behaviour in terms of mask helped him a great deal. The intercalation of different shades of feelings and ideas — some metaphoric and some otherwise in his poetry was essentially an off-shoot of mask-wearing intellectual exercise.

Richard Ellman has a perspicuous point of view when he comments 'In his devious way Yeats is coming at the problem of identity and is puzzling over such Questions as : Can we discuss a man apart from his dreams and aspirations? Carl a man think of himself without thinking of how he appears to others ? Is not every man an actor? who does not wear a mask? These are the relevant questions Yeats thought in his poetic career; and then, took pains to answer them. Yeats wrote in 1909, 'I think that all happiness depends on the energy to assume the mask of some other self; that all joyous or creative life is a re-birth as something not onself, something which has no memory and is created in a moment and perpetually renewed.' In another letter, he is more explicit: 'I want you to understand that once one makes a thing subject to reason, as distinguished from impulse, one plays with it, even if it is a very serious thing.... All my moral endeavour for many years has been an attempt to recreate practical instinct in myself. I can only conceive of it as of a kind of acting.'

Yeats was a poet who quested to texturise his wide experience in terms of his subjective insights and objective understanding of the world around him. His strategy of 'masks', his interest in myths and symbols along with his keen power of receptivity enabled him to produce poetry of striking freshness. Though in his early stage of his poetic career, he showed inadequate response to the role of reason in his life; but as he received emotive setbacks, he realised the importance of reason without in any way belittling the play of 'emotion and imagination to which he was instinctively drawn from his childhood.

The most characteristic feature of Yeats's poetry, both verse and drama, is that he was able to harmonise 'the aristocratic and highly conceptualised art of the symbolists to the legendary and mystical traditions of the Irish history, legend, or popular superstitions of the Irish folk.' 16In itself, it is a tremendous achievement. From Swedenborg, William Blake, Mall acme, Villiers de L'Isle-Adam and Materlinck, he learnt to treat poetry with hieratic significance, for the poet establishes relationship with the invisible.

From his writings, one can infer four major factors — one, his visionary temperament, his endeavour to harmonise carnality with spirituality, his abiding sense of being an Irish, and above all his sedulously cultivated belief in the special destiny of poet as the cracle of human race. These four factors quickened his creative imagination. In respect of the first constitutive element in Yeats's personality, it may be pointed out that his sense of the occult enabled him to go beyond the commonplace. The highly complex mind of Yeats reacted to carnal passion for Maud Gonne on a plane of sublimation, delicacy and idealism, as is borne out in a number of poems in which the chief motif centres around the fascinat-ing personality of this lady.

Maud Conne's influence on Yeats was tremendous indeed. For the poet, she had become a charismatic figure. It would not be farfetched to say that Maud Gonne had acquired a mythic status for the poet. in the last two lines of the poem, 'No second Troy' with Maud Gonne in background, Yeats mythologised her :

> Why, what could she have done
> being what she is ?
> was there another Troy for her
> to burn?

'No poet has celebrated a woman's beauty to the extent. Yeats did in his Lyric verse about Maud Gonne. From his second book to " 'Last Poems she becomes 'The Rose',

'Helen of Troy' (The Leden Body), Cathleen ni Houlihan, Pallas Athene, and Deirdre,"

She is the recurring theme in a number of poems under 'The Rose (1893) series, 'The wind among the Beasts (1899), 'In the Seven Woods (1904), 'The Green Helmet and other poems (1910), 'Responsibilities (1914)', 'The wild Swans at Coole (1919)', 'Michael Robartes and the Dancer (1921), 'The Tower (1923)', 'The Winding Stair and Other Poems (1933)' and 'Last Poems (1938-39)'. It appears that Yeats's mind got imaginatively alchemised whenever he remembered Maud Gonne; and in this process, her image acquired sublime identity. It is so in 'A Bronze Head' carrying a reference to Maud Gonne . The poet is almost ecstasied to express.

> Or else I thought her supernatural;
> As though a sterner eye looked through her eye
> on this foul world in its decline and fall,
> on gangling stocks grown great,
> great stocks run dry,
> Ancestral pearls all pitched into a sty,
> Heroic reverie mocked by clown and knave
> And wondered what was left for massacre to save.

Yeats is one of the few poets who believed in abiding friendship with talented men and women. Besides Maud Gonne who with her fascination had pulled Yeats to the Irish patriotic cause, Lady Augusta Gregory, Florence Farr and Mrs Olivia Shakespeare contributed a great deal in making Yeats a truly 'Yeatsian', for this was the poet who fused the contraries in his life experiences, and by doing so, he made his poems click and scintillate. In his poem, 'Friends', the poet remembers with delight his friendly association with Olivia Shakespeare (also called Diana Vernon), Lady Augusta Gregory and Maud Gonne:

> Now must I these three praise
> Three women that have wrought
> What joy is in my days

and with these introductory lines, the poet means to imply that each of them was a source of joy to him :

> How could I praise that one?
> when day begins to break
> I count my good and bad,
> Being wakeful for her sake,
> Remembering what she had,
> what eagle look still shows,
> While up from my heart's root
> So great a sweetness flows
> I shake from head to foot.

The words are simple and homely enough to evoke the feeling of innocence with which the poet inscribes his feelings with gratitude for his well-wishers. If Yeats had the benefit of diverse studies which helped him in modulating his poetic expression, he was also a man who cherished memories of his friends. No wonder that even at the Nobel Prize ceremony, Yeats in his simple-worded speech of acceptance chose to speak with gratitude of his friends who in one way or the other made him a great recipient of the Nobel prize in 1923:

Thirty years ago a number of Irish writers met together in societies and began a remorseless criticism of the literature of their country. It was their dream that by freeing it from provincialism they might win for it European recognition. I owe much to those men, still more to those who joined. our movement a few years later, and when I return to Ireland these men and women, now growing old like myself, will see in this great honor a fulfilment of that dream. I in my heart know how little I might have deserved it if they had never existed.

Yeats combined in himself the attributes of a great man and the talents of a studious scholar with sharp imagination; and necessarily, as a result of this 'alchemical' fusion in one person of diverse cultural elements, Yeats was able to mark out the progress of his poetry from one stage to another. Ttis involvement with different ,myths and symbols contributed a great deal in making his poetic expression run on different psychic wave-lengths whereby one is greatly charmed as also instructed to realize the complexity of this world and its beauties. Yeats along with T.S. Eliot and a very few artists in the twentieth century realized this basic existential truth of combinding personal integrity with imaginative creativity.

Yeats was the poet who developed a viable philosophy of life. As a result, he could maintain uninterrupted intellectual growth till the end of his life. His creativity over a span of at least five decades partly stemmed from his awareness of the occult. It meant the mythopoeic vision of man and his destiny. In his 'A Vision', he has touched upon man and the fact of his mortality. Death strikes terror in the heart of average man; but a true poet, as Yeats was, the haunting hump of a death is no problem. He develops the serenity of mind to enjoy the allotted life-span. One should have the cheerfulness of heart to prepare himself for the last hour. The last stanza of his poem, 'The Apparitions', bespeaks about Yeats's philosophical maturity :

When a man grows old his joy
Grows more deep day after day,
His empty heart is full at length
But he has need of all that strength
Because of the increasing Night
That opens her mystery and fright.
Fifteen apparitions have I seen;
The worst a coat upon a coat-hanger.

The underlined portion, repeated after every stanza in this poem, is illustrative of Yeats's dexterity to impart thematic seriousness by a slight quirk in thought-pattern.

With single-minded seriousness, Yeats undertook to discover areas of human experience. At the same time, he did net forget the law of limits for every domain of activity – intellectual, professional skills, business enterprise and others. The law of relativity rules all. As an artist, Yeats wanted to do justice to everything in dynamic ensemble. In this respect, he stood by the life.-principle, most vehemently expounded by D.H. Lawrence: 'Once and for all and for ever, let us have done with the ugly imperialism of any absolute. There is no absolute good, there is nothing absolutely right. All things flow and change, and even change is not absolute.'

Life, specially in its rarefied forms, reveals a picture of incongruous parts; and so it becomes exhaustive and burdensome to maintain high-minded seriousness all throughout for any pretty long time. Precisely, Yeats sometimes wrote poems in which there is a different flavour. It appears as if the poet was slightly disenchanted with his efforts to crystalise artistic permanence on a note of high tragedy. One such poem is 'High Talk'. In the first eight lines of this interesting poem, Yeats takes a slighting look at the social ways by which men and women try to show off and appear more than their intrinsic worth. Precisely, the poet in a humorous vein observes:

That patching old heels they may shriek,
I take to chisel and plane.
Malachi Stilt-Jack am I, whatever I
learned has run wild,
From collar to collar, from stilt to stilt,
from father to child.
All metaphor, Malachi, stilts and all.
A barnacle goose
Far up in the stretches of night; night
splits and the dawn breaks loose;
I, through the terrible novelty of light,

stalk on, stalk on;
Those great sea-horses bare their teeth
and laugh at the dawn.

It is a typical 'Yeatsian' poem in which the true morality of life is juxtaposed to the prevailing practices of the majority described in the preliminary phase of the poem. It is the working of thought-end-feeling dialectic that imparts a peculiar density to his verse. It does also show poet's power of apperception of the things around him. In the larger sense, he was liberal because he tried to take an all-sided view of reality. It does not mean that he had no convictions; rather the few that he had, he tried to nourish them with assiduous delicacy and care. If he was interested in the occult, he was also interested in the well-being of man without for-saking the occult side of human personality. His belief in friendship and love, already alluded to, was part of life's philosophy. It is in this background we can appreciate his poetic efforts to distil meaning out of his joining even incongruous ideas and feelings.

In terms of true life-span, he did not hesitate to revise his earlier opinion on any subject. 'For Victorian science and for realism in art he conceived what he calls 'a monkish hate'; and he began to feel that even his father sacrificed beauty too readily to realism.' 26 As he grew in experience and learning, he affirmed realism by broadening its narrow victorian concept. 'The extraordinary nature of his poetic vitality came from his ability to remodel his personality, perhaps even on a model which he had used before, but never quite in the 27 same way.' It is a sign of his being truly alive. The poet bore within himself an unageing thirst for life and its affirmations :

Grant me an old man's frenzy
Myself must I remake
Till I am Timon and Lear
or that William Blake
Who beat upon the wall
Till Truth obeyed his call. 28

His poetry was a battle-field for discovering his own self within all the devious contradictions in which he lived. He discovered himself by composing creative poetry. Richard Ellman observes on Yeats's life and poetry: "The principles of growth and of stability keep constant watch on one another in Yeats's poetry. He was a many-sided man who by dint of much questioning and inner turmoil achieved the right to speak with many voices and to know completely the incompleteness of life. And if, as seems likely, his work will resist time, it is because in all his shape-changing he remains at the centre tenacious, solid, a 'marble triton among the streams.'"

Yeats was a poet who thought and felt for himself. He did not accept anything, even the oracled one, without proper study and reflection. From 1920 onward till the second world war, Fascism had made inroads even in countries otherwise democratic. During this period, Yeats wrote and talked in terms of democracy being a spent-force. In some powerful sections of Irish and English public opinion, it was wrongly held that Yeats was a fascist. However, after taking all his pronouncements on contemporary politics, one can very well say that he was quite remote from advocating Fascism or Communism. The man who prized individual freedom and rebelled against any form of authoritarian thinking just could not give blind allegiance to Fascism and Dictator-ship. It is true that like all great artists he had fascination for aristocracy of intellect; and his advocacy of this point of view made him greatly misunderstood. on the other hand, Yeats had a terrible insight into different forms of revolution. His poem, 'The Great Day' is revealing enough to .be worth quoted to show that Yeats was not a facile political thinker. He had a grip on the processes that make civilisation and that unmake it.

Hurrah for revolution and more cannon shot;
A beggar upon horseback lashes a beggar upon foot;
Hurrah for revolution and cannon come again,
The beggars have changed places but the lash goes on.

Is it not true? Yeats had a grasp of cultural and political events around him. Even as Yeats's greatness as a poet was owing to his powerful imagination, he did not lose track of rational thinking. in his quest for a complete grasp of reality in all its manifoldness, he came to realize that man's experience would always remain incomplete even as it is true, one can have a better grasp of things by living fully in the midst of contradictions. 'Yeats suggests that we can express it through a series of contradictions. Here he is closer to Kierkegaard than is usually supposed. The principle involved is that the more sharply we represent the contradictions of life, the more urgently we invoke a pattern of the reality which must transcend then or include them. The poet cannot penetrate to the reality directly, but he can give a sense of the jaggedness and anfructuosity which it must encompass. Through focusing the contradictory attitudes which entrance his mind without securing its final allegiance, the poet presents reality as if by antithesis.' Here, it would be better to say that the poet presents reality by the sheer power of suggestiveness implied in any symbolic expression. In case of Yeats, such an assessment is aptly applicable.

Yeats's best poems are unique embodiments of truth. He admired Coleridge most who had also opined that 'truth is the correlative of being.' in point of reality, poet's knowledge is fundamentally personal and intuitive. It also implies that no truth exists independently of its embodiment. Any scholastic abstraction of thought was distrusted by Yeats; and he regarded such an approach merely rhetoric. He was firmly convinced that through reliance on abstract thought, one just cannot reach the portals of true poetry. It is true that Yeats did not disallow the role of rational thought, but it is just preparatory to serve as provender for the brain faculties to get intuitive apprehension. Yeats affirms this standpoint. In a letter to his father (12-9-1914), Yeats observed

> I think you that the poet seeks truth, not abstract truth, but a kind of vision of reality which satisfies the whole being. It will not be true for one thing unless it

> satisfies his desires, his most profound desires. Henry More, the seventeenth century Platonist whom I have been reading all summer, argues from the goodness and omnipotence of God that all our deep desires must be satisfied, and that we should reject a philosophy that does not satisfy them. I think the poet reveals truth by revealing those desires.

Yeats wrote with magical charm on these most profoundly dear to him. He wrote with consummating passion on Ireland and Irish themes. The last stanza of the poem 'The Statues' is one of which Yeats gets ecstasied on his being an Irish :

> When Pearse summoned Cuchulain to his side,
> What stalked through the Post Office?
> What intellect,
> What calculation, number, measurement,
> replied?
> We Irish, born into that ancient sect
> But thrown upon this filthy modern tide
> And by its formless, spawning, fury wrecked,
> Climb to our proper dark, that we may trace
> The lineaments of a plummet-measured face.

The Gyres' is such another poem in which the poets puts forth his deep-seated feelings on man's determination to retain his identity throughout the turbulence of times and the gyratory flux of events across a wide span of history. The first stanza is illustrative of Yeats's poetic calibre to fuse some of the major symbols and myths of the western world into a composite whole in which one finds the changing face of history :

> The gyres : the gyres : old Rocky Face
> look forth
> Things thought too long can be no longer
> thought
> For beauty dies Of beauty,worth of worth,
> And ancient lineaments are blotted out.
> Irrational streams of blood are staining earth;

Empedocles has thrown all things about;
Hector is dead and there's a light in Troy;
We that look on but laugh in tragic joy.

The last two lines of the second stanza may be excerpted here, for lack of space to convey Yeats's serenity of mind in accepting the fate with its turbulence in a mood of tragic joy: 'What matter? Out of Cavern comes a voice/And all it knows is that one word. 'Rejoice.' The last stanza of 'The Gyres' carries the flavour of the old Testament through which man becomes aware of the complexity of this universe in the sense that the life experiences gyrate around and in between the obnoxious and dark things, and men of celestial wisdom; but then again the gyre of history turns on to a new cycle of creation :

Conduct and work grow coarse, and
coarse the soul,
What matter Those that Rocky Face
holds dear,
Lovers of horses and of women, shall
From marble of a broken sepulchre
or dark betwixt the polecat and the owl,
or any rich, dark nothing disinter
The workman, noble and saint, and all
things run
on that unfashionable gyre again.

Enough has been projected in support of Yeats's greatness as a poet. However, his own epitaph from 'Under Ben Bulben' may be referred once again, as this book is in the process of being ended, to point out that Yeats as a poet believed in the impersonality of artist, like Ezra Pound and T.S. Eliot, for with this attitude, poetry is made free of the from somantic effusiveness. In this way, a poem serves as a milestone across the twilight terrain of culture and civilization. This is what the last stanza of this poem conveys :

Under bare Ben Bulben's head
In Drumcliff churchyard Yeats is laid,
An ancestor was rector there

Long years ago; a church stands near,
By the road an ancient Cross.
No marble, no conventional phrase,
on limestone quarried near the spot
By his command these words are cut :
Cast a cold eye
on life, on death.
Horseman, pass by.'

Yeats had a plethora of great sentiments; but at no stage, he was sentimental. He lived through difficulties problems and tensions with an impersonal serenity of a great thinker and philosopher; and as and when, he did express in them something memorable and abiding for readers to acknowledge on their own the greatness of W.B. Yeats as a poet who made a good use of symbols and mythological elements of Ireland and of other countries in his poetry and drama.